T0198641

PREVIOUS BOOKS

Healing by Contacting Your Cells.
Journal Excepts from the Ring of Fire.
What Can You Do To Help Our World?
2013 And Beyond.
2013 And Beyond Part II.
2014 World Journals.
2015 World Healing.
2015 World Healing II.
2016 World Journals.
2016 World Journals II.
Memories 2017.

http://www.globalmeditations.com

Note: http://www.globalmeditations.com opens with the book listing giving cover photos, chapter names, etc.

MEMORIES 2017 PART II

Barbara Wolf; Margaret Anderson

authorHOUSE®

AuthorHouse™
1663 Liberty Drive
Bloomington, IN 47403
www.authorhouse.com
Phone: 1 (800) 839-8640

Published by AuthorHouse 01/08/2018

ISBN: 978-1-5462-2359-7 (sc)
ISBN: 978-1-5462-2357-3 (hc)
ISBN: 978-1-5462-2358-0 (e)

Library of Congress Control Number: 2017910126

Photo taken by Victoria Lee of Mount Shasta.
Barbara is wearing a rose-colored sweater and Margaret
is wearing a blue jacket.

Print information available on the last page.

This book is printed on acid-free paper.

This book is dedicated to Barbara's husband Jack
and to the rest of the world.

ACKNOWLEDGEMENTS

Hideo Nakazawa
Masami Saionji
Chief Golden Light Eagle
Grandmother SilverStar
Divino Roberto Verissimo
Shishir Srivastava
Salwa Zeidan
Carmen Balhestero
David J. Adams
Victoria Lee
Mieko Sakai
Tim Janis
James Tyberonn
James Twyman
Sharon and Richard Van Duizend
Fumi Johns Stewart
Hiroyoshi Kawagishi
Mitsuru Ooba
Kazuyuki Namatame
Joe Roscoe
Sage Walker
Marco and Irene Hadjidakis
Peter and Judy Dix
Kim Reid
Annelis Kessler
Marilu Montenegro
Stella Edmundson
Robert Ziefel
Emma Kunz
Judy Moss

FOREWORD

We firmly believe in what we believe, and we realize you may not agree with everything we believe. Probably we would not agree with everything you agree with. But let us put aside our differences and let us be friends.

It's the world that matters. Mother Earth needs help and we are trying to give it to her. That is all that is expected.

CONTENTS

INTRODUCTION

Chapter 1. We take you to powerful Mount Shasta in northern California to prepare for big energies coming to the Earth.

Chapter 2. Then, a rare Total Eclipse will cross the North American continent and greatly diminish energy. We need to increase it.

Chapter 3. The Healing Light Group invites us to attend a sacred bonfire. Afterward, we drive to a sacred lake to take in its powerful energies.

Chapter 4. Because there are many Healers and Spiritual Beings associated with this planet, we give you a description of several, including Braco who sends healing energy by gazing rather than speaking. Many claim to have been healed.

Chapter 5. Famous Yellowstone takes our interest because it contains sacred water that has healing properties. There are fourteen sacred springs around the world and we name them and their location. Since they all have a consciousness, we join them together so their combined powerful energy will help the world.

Chapter 6. The Pacific has been rumbling with volcanoes and earthquakes. Specifically, we put our attention on two places—Mount Agung on the island of Bali in Indonesia and on Vanuatu, an island complex suspected of being associated with the tremendous 2011 earthquake off Japan that ruined a vast nuclear power plant which is still spewing nuclear waste into the Pacific.

Chapter 7. While writing our book, North Korea has shot a missile over neighboring Japan. It landed in the Pacific. This action and other recent testing has greatly disturbed the Japanese. Our thoughts are on stopping aggression and increasing peace. We have included information in this chapter about Margaret's aunt and uncle who helped Korean refugees after the Korean war of the 1950's.

Chapters 8 & 9. Now we put our attention on our journey to the United Arab Emirates and to India where we speak at an annual gathering of Chief Justices of the world. Earlier, we have spoken at other annual India conferences and we enjoy speaking as well as visiting India and neighboring United Arab Emirates.

Chapters 10 & 11. Our book ends with a journey to New York City where we attend a fantastic concert performed by Tim Janis and others at Carnegie Hall. Then we go to the 9/11 Tribute Museum to concentrate on patching religious differences so that another 9/11 will not happen. Our third event in New York City is to attend a Brooklyn Tabernacle gathering of 2,000 people singing with their hearts full of love.

CHAPTER 1

Mount Shasta

F rom Barbara:

Our journey will be to sacred, powerful Mount Shasta in northern California. We have bought our air tickets and we leave August 6, returning August 10. The big moment will be August 8, called 8-8, when powerful energies are coming to Earth. The Lion's Gate will be open.

What is the Lion's Gate? It is the opening of a portal where huge energy will come in because there are three powerful alignments happening. These three are the earth, the sun, and Sirius which, at that moment, is the brightest star in the sky. The earth will be receiving powerful Light energy from the power of the sun and Sirius at that time. If we realize this, we can align ourselves with this positive energy to send it out from the West to East as we fly home.

From Margaret:

In order to prepare for my journey for next week to Mount Shasta, I connect to Mount Shasta who answers me.

Sacred Flames burn here beneath the surface. The Flame of Resurrection. The Flame of Healing. The Flame of Love. Mother Earth's heart is close to the surface here. The mountains were created by her internal fire. Take the Shasta Frequency and make it your own. Peace and Beauty, Love, Harmony and Healing.

So many gather here to drink the pure water, the pure love of the mountain, distant yet close. Always present. An honor to be here. The doors are always open. Think on Shasta and you are here. The frequency influence of Shasta is worldwide – planetary.

The basic frequency of Light (Life) is Love. Carry that through your life. That is the heart song of the humans. Love is the basic principle of creation. You saw the wonder of the Milky Way. That was my gift to you and to the group. Each one will receive more gifts as they give their gifts. Each giving one is a fountain of Joy and Harmony and Love – Light – Peace.

Peace, Love and Light.

Blessings from Shasta.

———————

Another channeling:

Radiating Love that heals. It is all very simple. The animals, birds, and sea creatures do it naturally. Their instinct is to love, to create. Humanity is more complex. Their thoughts shade the expression of love. Sometimes it becomes lost or dim but it reignites again. It is always there, the core principle, LOVE.

Blessings from Shasta. We are always with you in peace and in love.

———————

August 6:

Breakfast at 4:00 a.m., and then Joan the taxi driver comes at 5:00 a.m. to take us to the airport to go to Mount Shasta. Our first flight is to Chicago.

My seatmate is a young Chinese male student aged fifteen from Xi'an, and I enjoy talking with him. He is on a tour seeing Yellowstone,

Niagara Falls, Hawaii. Wow. He says, in China students go to school from 7:00 a.m. to 7:00 p.m., six days a week. His favorite subject is math and paper and pencil are used for calculations. He has an iPhone. He also loves music and he plays a guitar. His favorite sport is soccer. In fact, he is a goalie. We enjoy our conversation.

On arrival in Chicago, I disembark and say good-bye to my new friend.

Here, Barbara and I transfer to a plane bound for Denver, Colorado, and then another plane to Medford, Oregon where we will spend the night. Mount Shasta is our goal for the next day.

————————

August 7:

Today is the day of the Lunar Eclipse, 3:11 a.m. Mountain Time, 6:11 a.m. my body time. I celebrate it with my mind.

When it is time to leave the hotel, we rent a car and begin driving toward Mount Shasta. The roads are strong and curving and we go a long way up mountains and a long way down mountains. There is a forest fire haze but we do not see the fire.

Then, at a distance we see Mount Shasta and we also see Black Butte Mountain standing as Shasta's sentinel. When we reach the busy city of Mount Shasta, we make our way to the Visitor's Center. Here, we see three new Peace Poles standing at the entrance welcoming everyone coming to Shasta.

We phone Victoria Lee to have lunch with us and she agrees, saying afterwards she will drive us up the mountain. And yes, the drive up is amazing. We have learned that the upper drive has been closed to protect delicate spring flowers appearing now that the snow is melting. Later, we realize we are some of the first visitors to reach the top of the Mount Shasta's parking area. WOW!

This is the cover of our book.

Mount Shasta speaks to me:

The Great Mountain of Shasta welcomes you. That is why people stand in awe of the Mountain – the vastness, the presence of Mother Earth's heart.

Lighten your load. Come without agenda. Come as Spirit.

The layers of Lemuria are here,* The Pacific rim, the beginning of the great continent that is here in everyone's frequency.

*See Glossary: The Lemurian community of Telos beneath Mount Shasta.

Softness, quietness, sweetness, gentleness, strength, focus, peace— allowance of all to grow and be nourished.

Nature is Glory. Nature is profound. You are a leaf waving on a branch—part of the whole. The Great Drama of Life on the Planet.

Move out to this wonderful day. You were already here before you left your home.

Love from Mount Shasta.

———————

At the parking area near the top of Mount Shasta, I ring the Blessings Chimes* for the mountain to acknowledge the great presence and power of Shasta. I walk to little flowers and draw with my finger Vortex Symbols * on a recording stone beside the flowers. The stone feels pleased. I can see faint Symbols seemingly already there.

*See Glossary: Blessings Chimes.
*See Glossary: Vortex Symbols.

I offer the Vortexes to Mount Shasta and to the Lemurians living beneath Shasta. Also, I offer the Vortexes to the Sun and to the Whales and Dolphins who are present but in a higher dimension.

The wind comes up. And the Sun comes out!! I hold out the open first page of my Vortex booklet to the Galactic entities above and I say, "These are your Symbols!"

The Elements of Water, Fire, Land, Air, etc. receive and acknowledge the Vortexes. The wind blows. The clouds part to greet the Sun. The sun shines brightly, highlighting Light.

Now, cloud dragons appear in the sky overhead and whale and dolphin clouds appear.

———————

As Victoria drives us down Shasta, I continue wondering about this magical mountain. Trees welcome us. Wild flowers, purple, white, yellow abound.

Shasta is happy.

While on the mountain, I have a feeling of the closeness other worlds, of Brothers and Sisters from other galaxies,

———————

August 8:

We have breakfast with Victoria at the Black Bear Diner which has delicious home-cooked food plus a MAGNIFICENT VIEW of Mount Shasta whose presence is expansive and powerful!!!

After breakfast we go to the nearby Visitor's Center to photograph the three Peace Poles for friends in Japan who strongly promote Peace Poles for the world.

Then we drive to the nearby Gateway Peace Garden to visit Mother Mary's meditation garden. Mount Shasta is in view. We feel great peace here and the feeling of the Divine Feminine. Many flowers surround Mary. Nearby we visit another Peace Pole location where we quietly sit in peace.

A bit further along, we visit the Quan Yin Meditation Garden that has prayer ties clustered on oak trees embracing the loving statue of Quan Yin. This garden is also serene and peaceful.

I softly ring the Blessings Chimes in front of Quan Yin, and Victoria says she can see Quan Yin's smile deepen.

———————

Just after 12 noon, we drive to McCloud Middle Falls that has a HIGH VIEW, SPECTACULAR VISTA of the river snaking below. I ring the Blessings Chimes for the water, for the trees, for the rocks.

People are swimming off the rocks—humans in league with the mountain water – others perched on rocks and some diving off high rocks into deep pools.

We then drive to McCloud Upper Falls where I see amazing vegetation— large circular plant clusters. Beautiful!! They are Indian rhubarb.

I am with Victoria where we see the Indian rhubarb, and now we return to Barbara who is sitting at a picnic table with a group of French Canadians and Europeans. When we return to the car, Victoria says they are part of the French Canadian Telos Group. We know the city of Telos is in a higher dimension below Mount Shasta and so we immediately return and say hello to the Telos group. They light up with joy. They want to know about us and we hug and kiss. We say we will meet each other in Telos tonight.

———————

In the evening, Mount Shasta speaks again:

The Mountain is the Light of the world, much like Mount Fuji for the Japanese. There is a softness about the frequency of the people reflecting the Lemurian vibration of the heritage of the area.

The Sun Disc here expands and moderates the frequencies — the Atlantean Crystal of OM that moderates dimensions and time. Telos stands as a Beacon of Light to return to. It is the operating system– kindness and compassion – inclusiveness – operating from heart space rather than head space.

If you can take on the wonder of the mountain's presence, you can step into the wonder presence of the Milky Way and the multiple universes to become lost in the vastness.

Light and Love, that is the operating system of Shasta.

There are Lines of entry – the Mary Line, the Quan Yin Line, the Telos Line, the Galactic Line – the cloud line, the fairy line – the angelic line, the Masters Line.

Sacred Geometry. Water.

————————

Later I receive channeling from Telos:

Knock, knock at the Door of Telos. *Yes, come in to share in the peace and vibration of Telos where all are equal in gifts and duties. Each offers his or her own talents to the whole.*

Telos stands ready to accept whoever knocks at our door. You may enter through the heart. Your credentials are that you are a seeker, creator, lover and healer. The heart frequency opens the door.

The greeting is the smile that lights the way to open the path from one to another. To share, to sing, to join together, is the Lemurian way of living.

The Planet is revered and cherished. Mother Earth, Mount Shasta and other sacred places are deeply held in one's Soul and cherished.

The ticket to Mother Earth is rare enough. The ticket to Shasta rarer still.

The ticket to Telos is quite rare. Only given to those who seek, who resonate with the core principles of the Telos communities. No ego. No agenda. Just openness and giving.

To share in the wondrous gift of living on Mother Earth, send your own positive energies for the maintenance of the Health Life Stream of the planet.

The crystals give Light to the health of the planet — created by fire to come to the surface to sustain and enhance the power of Mother Earth.

Humanity needs to give as much as it takes. Admiration, sending Love, sending Light, offering thanksgiving for the strength and beauty of the Great Mountain of Shasta. Thanksgiving to the tiniest plant, to the grandest tree – from the rock sand pebbles to the greatest boulder – from the drop of water to the roaring swift moving stream which forms a great river to flow to the ocean.

Water nourishes Life. Telos nourishes Life by sustaining the High Principles of Life Existences.

To float and not to strain. To give, to share freely of oneself. To walk with respect on Mother Earth's surface. To cherish all forms of Life, each equal in their worth and existence on the planet.

No one better than the other. All are the same in Creator's eyes. Everyone has a say. Everyone has life to enjoy to the fullest. A great symphony of joy rises up for the Vision of Mount Shasta growing larger and larger in wonder and power. Each being offering a gift to the whole.

This is from your friends from Telos. You are sitting with us – heart to heart, mind to mind, no separation. Love dissolves barriers.

Love and Life – free gifts to all life on the planet. Enjoy. Spread your Light.

Spread your Love. The world is enhanced by your presence – everyone's presence.

The mountain gives strength and Light. The power expands. The Planet is enhanced. All are lifted up to a higher dimension.

This is Shasta and why everyone is drawn here.

AUM.

_____

August 9:

In the early morning at sunrise, Victoria again takes us to the top of Mount Shasta. When we reach the top, we see a Native American drumming and singing traditional songs. We move to a nearby picnic table where I ring the Blessings Chimes.

A great hawk circles above us.

_____

August 10:

Now it is time for us to fly across the country giving out peace energies. The Lion's Gate is still open. In addition to North America, we also focus on Peace and Healing for the world.

CHAPTER 2

Solar Eclipse

F rom Barbara:

August 21, a total Solar Eclipse will cross the North American continent. This will happen because the position of the moon crosses in front of the sun and diminishes the light. In the old days, and even in some places today, eclipses were feared because of the sun disappearing. It is thought that this is a bad omen.

I realize there can be a momentary lessening of the energy of the sun during an eclipse and it is time to roll up my sleeves before an eclipse to help increase energy when it will fade for a moment.

Shasta becomes the major Sun Disc to be considered when the Eclipse begins crossing North America. It is the first North American Sun Disc to be touched by the diminishment, the lessening of sun energy on the continent.

Pinnacle Mountain of Arkansas controls the Sun Discs of North America. We need to ask the entities in charge of the world Sun Discs to help increase Light energy at Pinnacle Mountain which controls the Sun Discs of North America. Automatically, when the Pinnacle Sun Disc energy is increased, this will increase the Light energy on all the Sun Discs of North America, including the Shasta Sun Disc.

The major Sun Disc of the world is at Rosslyn Chapel, Scotland.

We need to ask for help from the guardians of this major world Sun Disc. They have known me for twenty years. I need to share with them my thoughts of constantly energizing Light during the time of maximum Eclipse.

Yes, we are busy preparing for the Eclipse. And we have been contacting people who can help. We have phoned Germany and Switzerland and we have notified Kim of Canada and Victoria Lee of Mount Shasta.

Then we drive a short way to Mendon Ponds which has powerful positive energy built up over millions of years when Mother Earth only experienced positive energies. As the Eclipse is in full force, we will send this positive energy across the North America. Especially, we will send it to Shasta.

——————————

Also from Barbara:

August 21:

I wake at 6:30 a.m. after a good night's sleep. Today is the beginning of the Eclipse and the daylight shows me a clear sky, cool, 63 degrees Fahrenheit, a slight breeze. I turn on soft music, dress, and then put in my hands a North American Sun Disc map showing twelve locations. I speak to the guardians of Rosslyn Chapel and ask them to join me in concentrating on giving powerful Light to these twelve locations.

I know the Eclipse will not touch the North America continent for several hours. Rochester, New York State, our location, is far from Mount Shasta where people will begin meditating at 12:06 p.m., the moment the Eclipse appears.

Margaret and I closely watch the time. When it arrives, we are expecting enormous power because of the number of people sending positive energy to counter the Eclipse. And yes, the positive energy is ENORMOUS. It shakes us to our roots. We had not realized it would be so huge.

We know the Eclipse will not reach our area for a time. We watch the clock, and when the Eclipse begins to come close, we look out the windows to see a multitude of leaves happily basking in the sun. These leaves show little movement. The wind has diminished to almost nothing and the sun is still shining brightly on the leaves.

At. 2:00 p.m., the wind completely stops. Now the sky is not dark, but the sun does not shine. The Eclipse is here. We watch, and when the Eclipse is over, the quiet leaves begin to slightly move. But the energy feels low. I continually send out the words of Love, Love, Love. Although I know the biggest love energy comes from the sun, it remains low, so I must substitute by saying the words over and over again — Love, Love, Love.

The daylight continues to remain dull. Not dark, not overcast. Within me, I see WHITE LIGHT. My body is White Light. I know powerful positive energies have been spread across the land. I know we can expect changes for the Earth because of an Eclipse, but I also know that many, many across the world have injected a flow of positive energy into this disruption.

Also, by means of Sun Discs, I know the Rosslyn Chapel guardians have used massive Light energy coming from those meditating to help spread powerful energy across the world.

———————————

Two days later, August 23, the world is still reeling from the massive energy sent out at the time of the Solar Eclipse. We know sound is a method to normalize the energy lines, the Songlines* of the world.

*See Glossary: Songlines.

These energy lines run here and there, above and below and within Mother Earth. They are all important energizers.

To help matters, we play the music of Tim Janis* and we tell the Rosslyn entities we are using this music sound to help normalize the energy lines — the all-important Songlines of the world.

*See Glossary: Tim Janis, "Flower Canyon" Music.

————————

Margaret's account of the Solar Eclipse:

August 20, we are approaching the Solar Eclipse when the sunlight is closed and reopens. It is a drama of Light and Darkness showing how fragile life is. How temporary, and yet eternal.

A comment from crystals:

The crystals are long-livers, millions of years old. Humans are like a wisp of time. From the crystal bedrock, we have seen the Solar Eclipse many times — held in our memories.

————————

August 21, beginning of the day of the Eclipse:

Father Sun says: *Blessings to the Earth inhabitants. The crystals are attuned to the Sun. They give their power to Mother Earth through the crystalline grid. Come join the grid. Plug into the grid through Love.*

————————

Before the Eclipse, Barbara has asked the Sun Disc entities of Rosslyn Chapel, Scotland to help. They say: *We will focus with you on the power of the Sun Discs — world wide and specific to that area of concern. The energy of the Sun Discs balances Mother Earth's grid and the people who live on the surface.*

Increase Light for the Sun Discs. Increase Love for the people – the inhabitants of the planet – human, animal, bird, plant, trees.

————————

I have been concerned about fires near Mouth Shasta. The Rosslyn Chapel entities respond:

The energy of the Sun Disc mountain (Mount Shasta) is powerful and is not affected by fire or temperature, rain or snow. We send tempering energy for the diminishment of fire. Focus on Light, Love. Remove attention to fire – that will slow down without attention. Moisture is expressed through love, balance, moderation. That is our essence, our job core.

––––––––––––

When the Eclipse begins in the Pacific, I sit with all my crystals at the window focusing on the light, on my breath, feeling the unification of the world in meditation. This reminds me of when everyone prayed for the astronauts of Apollo 13 to return from their moon mission in April of 1970.

When the Eclipse begins touching Rochester, New York State, I ring the Blessings Chimes for the Sun, Moon and Earth. Ringing, ringing, ringing.

The feeling tone is calm. I feel the world is with us witnessing this historic event – the diminishment of the Sun's Light and then the return of the Sun's Light.

As the Eclipse advances, the Sun's Light is becoming gradually dim, more opaque, like a curtain going down, or like seeing the scenery through a screen or through dark glasses. I feel a softness and yet, a heaviness.

Barbara and I discuss whether there is a change in the density of brightness of color outside. The dimming of sunlight is gradual. Now there is no sunlight on the leaves. It feels as if a storm is coming but there is no storm. The heart seeks the Light. All life turns to the Sun and now there is diminishment of Light. There is no joy. Where is the joy? Where is the Light? I yearn for the return of the Sun. I have to keep breathing and not to hold my breath. I breathe slowly, sending joy, sending love, sending Light.

When the sun comes back, I see movement of the leaves. Love, Love, Love. The energy will come back. I ring the Blessings Chimes for the return of the Light.

Slowly, it returns. Birds begin to sing. When the sun is out, I am happy. It is the end of the Eclipse.

We drive to Mendon Ponds to ring the Blessing Chimes at the water's edge while facing the Sun to send Blessings to the Sun, to the Earth, to the Moon for this special day.

AUM.

————————

After the Eclipse, Barbara says she begins wondering whether it has affected the Songlines of the world. These energize the world by running here, there, and everywhere.

The Higher Worlds say:

Light, Sound and Vibration.

Twelve major Sun Discs were energized to counterbalance the diminishment, blockage of the Sun's Light, Life force, and Love.

The major Songlines also need to be acknowledged for energizing Mother Earth. When the Songlines come together with each other, they form Power Nodes of Harmonic energy.

For humans to understand this, it opens the awareness of the energy flow for Earth healing. Awareness is energy exchange. Awareness is giving and receiving Light.

I ask, are the Songlines connected to the Earth's Crystalline Grid?

I am answered: *The Songlines are part of the crystalline grid and more. These are Earth energy currents.*

You have used the Vortexes to bring in off-world energy which affects the Earth, humans, animal life forms, etc.

Songlines are Earth energy currents. Sun Discs increase/decrease Earth's energy, grid, and life forms. Vortexes give energy and balance.

———————————

One of the Songlines is marked by a horse sculpture at Sundown Hill, Australia.* It is the crossing point of major Songlines.

*See Glossary: Horse Sculpture, Sundown Hill, Australia.

The Higher Worlds say, *Margaret, let the Horse energy line speak.*

The Horse energy line is expanded by the Power of the Solar Eclipse.

You saw the expansion of Power of Mount Shasta even before the Eclipse.

Humanity is expanding in consciousness with the decrease in ego and petty agenda. Consciousness expands when life is cherished. All forms of life are cherished, honored, blessed by Love. Expansion of Love is true horse power. A great healer.

Each Songline carries special energies. They are waiting for your understanding and recognition in your mind, heart, spirit. The energy connect has been lit! The Solar Eclipse opens the receptivity to receive this awareness. Welcome to the Songlines!

Use the Songlines, use the Vortexes, use the Sun Discs for energy expansion. Give Love to Mother Earth through all three systems.

You are a feeder line to turn onto the energy present here. You are a key giver – opening the doors of wisdom chambers held in Mother Earth's heart. Guarded and kept by the Crystals. All are connected.

The Songlines give energy to Mother Earth. The Sun Discs give energy to Mother Earth. The Vortexes give energy to Mother Earth.

With love from the Horse and the Higher Worlds.

CHAPTER 3

Sacred Fire ~ Sacred Lake

Just after the August Solar Eclipse, our friend Joe Roscoe invites us to a fire ceremony gathering of a group called the Healing Light Group. Although this ceremony will not be at the moment of the Solar Eclipse, it is still powerful.

We have never attended a Healing Light Group ceremony and so we do not know what to expect. Margaret channels Emma Kunz,* former healer, artist, whether or not we should go.

*See Glossary: Emma Kunz.

Emma responds: *Yes, a good idea to expand the Light force field. Give Shasta influence to the group. They will give you Arkansas influence.*

We know Mount Shasta has been the first powerful place to receive the Solar Eclipse energy when it reached the North American continent. We also know that members of Healing Light Group are influenced by powerful Arkansas crystals.

————————

Joe Roscoe kindly offers to drive us to the gathering and we agree and thank him. Immediately after our agreement, the Higher Worlds urge us to immediately find the place. We do not know that Joe Roscoe does not know the route. We say nothing to him, but we investigate immediately. When we locate the place via the Internet, we realize there must be confusing street signs. Well, we will go immediately, and if we become confused, we will stop and ask.

The day is sunny and beautiful as we drive quickly to reach our destination.

When signposts become confusing, we stop to ask directions from a man just leaving his house to enter his car. When we give him our destination and tell him we are puzzled, he smiles and says others are puzzled, too.

He points to his neighbor's yard which has been lawn mowed by a woman and he says she mowed the wrong grass. Street signs had confused her and when she was ready to mow another yard of grass, the man told her she was ready to mow another wrong grass! Yes, street signs had confused her.

Well, this man gives us directions to our destination and we carefully follow them.

August 26:

Later, when Joe Roscoe is driving us to the gathering, he becomes confused because he does not know how to reach our destination. He follows our directions and we arrive without a problem. Thank you, Higher Worlds, for telling us to drive earlier!

When we reach the place, we leave the car and walk behind a small house to sit with people who have already started a small fire. They are members of the Healing Light Group.

We join the circle and feel welcomed. The feeling of love is great and we know everyone is sharing love for Mother Earth, her crystals, her crystalline grid system, and her elements of air, land, water, fire. Yes, we are within a powerful energy field here with the group.

All are urged to speak, and Sage Walker, a member, says the Higher Worlds have wanted us to come to join in the fire ceremony. We say that at this moment we are concentrating on the elements of air, land, water, and fire because these elements feel the consequence of an unnatural use of Nature's elements. We speak about the need to heal the waters of the Pacific, home of the dolphins and whales and many sea creatures. Others speak about the use of crystals for healing the self and the planet.

When the fire is smartly glowing, each person takes a stick to hold prayers for Mother Earth. Then the stick is put into the fire to get rid of radiation, pollution, aggression, war, inequality. The Fire Element transforms the negative energy.

We are then given water to add to our prayers for healing the body and the planet.

Although we are strangers to this group, our energy comes together through the love of Mother Earth, the healing of her elements and the supporting of the quality of her life and well-being.

As we part, we feel Mother Earth's Light has strengthened from the friendship and prayers given here.

—————————

August 27:

The next morning, our attention is on the water element and we drive three plus hours to a sacred lake at the foothills of the Adirondacks Mountains.

This lake is one mile long and was formed 10,000 years ago by glaciers. Today it is fed by underground springs.

Our friends Sharon and Richard Van Duizend have a home overlooking this lake and they have invited us to visit them. The house sits on a high embankment with curving steps descending to the water. Their family has lived here for generations and they tell us why the lake is so important. It has been kept free of motorized boats and all machinery to prevent pollution. Respect for the water has full attention. No one living there can think otherwise.

─────────

From Margaret:

The afternoon is bright and clean when we arrive, and the lake is calm. I ring the Blessings Chimes for the lake and for all the plants and trees surrounding it. Dragonflies abound. Sharon, guardian of the lake, sounds the OMs to honor its beauty and purity. The water is shining, and the sun's face is reflected on the water. Fire and water are merged and healing. In the water, I begin drawing Vortex Symbols with a long narrow stick.

Now the wind picks up and the water ripples and sparkles. This is Light dancing on the water.

I draw the Whale Symbol of the Universal Law of Movement and Balance and the wind acknowledges this symbol. When I draw the Symbol of the Universal Law of Symmetry, the underground springs rise up to send currents of water to join in the celebration. Wind currents and spring currents cross each other to make diamond patterns. I also draw the Universal Law of Innocence, Truth, and Family as well as the Universal Law of Change. Now the dragonflies move back and forth and birds call out. The wind blows softly as I draw the powerful Universal Law of Nature, the Universal Law of Love and the Spiritual Law of Healing.

All of Nature is present when the lake is receiving this powerful energy. A great blue heron flies close to the water. We feel grateful to be present at this sacred place.

─────────

Still from Margaret:

August 28, 4:00 a.m. I am in bed and the Lake speaks to me.

Come into the water to be healed. Unnecessary thoughts leave behind. Striving, searching put aside. Here you meet the Essence of Water. Blessing water. Healing water. Dancing water. Reflective water. Love water enhancing life in the surroundings, in the region, in the Adirondacks, in the Niagara Escarpment.

The Ocean in my mind speaks: *The Lake dances. Because of the movement of the water, the Sun delights in all the sparkles produced. These are mirrors reflecting the Sun's grandeur and presence. The Lake is a good friend, companion, listener, reflector, Love absorber, Love giver.*

The Lake speaks: *My gift is the strength of Peace Vibration. Go in Peace, my dear friend. Come in Peace. Return again and again in your thoughts and delight. This is my essence. This is water and land and life on your Mother Earth planet. Cherish it. Creation is here to live and to contemplate with love.*

The Guardian of the Lake.

————————

From Barbara:

I am putting my attention on two elements, fire and water, to help Mother Earth and all her inhabitants — humanity, nature, animals, birds.

Just over a week ago, August 21, we experienced a very powerful Solar Eclipse. This brought much energy to Mother Earth. This energy is beneficial for helping to make changes, such as the ascension of Mother Earth and all living on her. However, changes signal a warning of imbalance.

 Just now, I realize the imbalance of fierce fires in the western area of the North American continent. Also, a fierce tropical storm is causing enormous amounts of water to invade the land in Texas, the southern part of North America.

Yes, I feel these are two imbalances that need to be addressed by humanity. As for myself, while attending the bonfire of the Healing

Light Group, we have addressed the Fire Element as a friend. We have come to the fire as friends.

Now I have addressed as a friend the out-of-control fires in the far west of the continent. The fire has a mind. It understands. Friends do not fight each other.

One time, in the southern part of South America, I walked in the evening to a bonfire where a nearby bench was set up for healing. A woman was lying on this bench and a healer was attending to her.

I knew the fire was being used to heal and I did not want to interfere with this. And so I moved away about thirty feet to sit on the ground and watch the fire/healing. But, I was not satisfied because I was too far away from the benefits of fire. Then, to my surprise, the fire spoke to me, saying, "You can be close to me or far, far away. It does not matter. I am always with your thoughts."

This pronouncement has stayed with me.

At the Healing Light Group bonfire, I put my thoughts on the need to temper the problem of fire on the North American continent. I know the fire is listening to me and I ask the fire to help balance Mother Earth.

————————

I have also worked with the water element which has a mind. Since the Solar Eclipse, there has been an imbalance of this element in south Texas.

As just mentioned, the place has been inundated with massive amounts of water. I ask the water to join forces with me to help stop out-of-control water and fire.

When I am at the pure lake near the Adirondacks Mountains, I watch the water at my feet and I see only small movement of tiny waves. But, when the sun is ready to go down for the evening, at certain moments, the sunlight touches the water and this forms patches of tiny sparkles on the water. They look like sparkling crystals. I call them 'sparklees'.

Again, I remember what the fire has told me — no matter how far away I am, the fire is with me. The water is the same as the fire. It is with me. With my mind, I am taking the pure water sparklees, and I am sending their pure energy to the out-of-control fires of North America. For the balance of Mother Earth.

————————

From Margaret:

When we leave the sacred lake, my mind is still on FIRE and WATER.

I understand Barbara's concentration to calm the water in Texas. Also, the water in the Gulf of Mexico. Both places are experiencing turmoil because of hurricanes.

As we begin driving home, we listen to calm music on the car's CD player.

We use this healing sound to give healing water energy to Texas and Gulf of Mexico from the sacred Adirondacks lake. I think of the Light sparkles on the sacred lake. This is Life Force within the water, and so I cap this positive energy over the entire region of Texas and the Gulf of Mexico.

But, at the same time I am thinking of the importance of water—Life Creation, Life Sustaining. I am beginning to worry a bit about the sacred lake. Are we pulling off its energies too much?

The Sacred Lake responds:

Like fire, I am an eternal source of healing. I am the Niagara Escarpment. I am the Sacred Springs. I provide the mirror for the Sun Light to dance upon the water to make the sparkles.

You do not need to worry about the diminishment of energy. The Water Element is eternal. The Fire Element is eternal. My Love, My

Being, is eternal. Your Love, your Being, is eternal. It is just what perspective is used.

Honor Sharon who is guarding the water and the Light. You work with my Light in full glory. Work also with the Love and Light from other dimensions – the Elementals, the Angels, the Masters.

Sit and understand the essence of the lake. The water, the stones, life forms of standing tall trees. Enjoy.

Feel the beauty. Feel the healing. Feel the Joy which is my love.

Creation is here to live and to contemplate with love.

Go in Peace, my dear friend.

With love,

The Guardian of the Lake.

Chapter 4

Healers And Spiritual Beings

Braco

From Barbara:

For several years via the computer, Margaret and I have been speaking to PAX TV, a peace center in Brazil. Owner Carmen Balhestero speaks to us by SKYPE and we can see each other. She records our talks and weekly transmits them to the world.

Behind us are spiritual beings whose pictures are facing the computer as we talk to her. None of them are living today, but we know them from their pictures. This chapter will tell you about these spiritual ones and others.

One spiritual being is Braco, still living and working in the third dimension of our world. At posted times, via the Internet, he gazes at the world. It is free and anyone can look at him. He is a healer and many who look at him claim they have been healed by his gaze.

With only a slight smile on his face, Braco remains silent while gazing. Some call him the Gazer. My feeling is that people should look at his gazing face which is one hundred percent healthy. Healthy Braco is full of love for all looking at him. We have been hearing about those whose illness has been removed and replaced by health free of disease.

Braco is from Croatia and one time he came to our location for the witnessing of his gazing.

————————

From Margaret:

When Braco came to Rochester, I helped with the publicity of telling the people. I was delighted that many, many came.

When he was gazing, I saw his strong loving presence that the people silently and intensely took in. Everyone was joined in a single focus of gazing, receiving his healing. The energy level was high. Afterward, the people spoke about this as they carried away Braco's positive healing energy.

During one of his gazing programs on the computer, a man spoke about how he was in the hospital with a stroke that had left him unable to speak. A computer was brought to his room where he watched Braco gazing, and then the man began to speak. He told us this incident and tears were brought to our eyes.

This year, October 11, when I watched Braco gazing on the computer, we were told that the eyes of people in sixty-seven countries were on his gaze. I watched as he seemed to gaze and lock into the eyes of the people. I waited, and when I saw he had locked into my gaze, I felt enormous energy of love coming to me. My cells were all at attention, soaking up the divine healing Love projected by him. I thanked Braco.

Bruno Groening

From Barbara:

And now we will tell you about Bruno Groening who was born in 1906 and died in 1959. His knowledge of healing was so famous, people world wide came to his German residence to be healed. Daily, an estimated 30,000 gathered outside his residence. He was called a Miracle Doctor who believed a higher power, 'Heilstrom', could heal. His emphasis rested on the need for all to trust and to believe in the divine power. A person needed to be spiritually open.

It was quite by accident that Margaret and I learned about Bruno Groening. We picked up a brochure about him that was mingled with about a dozen other brochures. This brochure told us there would be a local gathering to learn about heath and healing on the spiritual path through the teaching of Bruno Groening. We did not even know his name, but the invitation seem interesting.

The gathering place was in a library easy to reach. At the appointed hour, we arrived at the library and we were told that the meeting was in a special room on the first floor. The door to the room was closed, and when we opened it, we discovered two people, a man and a woman, seated at a very small table that held a video projector.

We waited for others to come but none came. And so, we sat at the tiny table with the other two and watched an hour-long video about Bruno Groening. It took only a moment to realize we were looking at a very special man.

The video is being shown in many places in North America. An organization, the Bruno Groening Circle of Friends, shows this video.

Another group, a medical scientific group, spreads news about the healing, and yes, a large number of healings have been reported.

Carmen Balhestero

From Barbara:

As mentioned earlier, we are friends with Carmen Balhestero who lives in Brazil and who is in charge of a Peace Center called PAX Center. She has been inviting us to speak to her via SKYPE. As we speak, she translates our English words into Portuguese, and then our talk is sent out to the world via her computer network.

Carmen has a close connection with Saint Germain, and he often gives in English a short comment or two before Carmen asks us to speak.

In September, Margaret channeled Saint Germain, and he said:

Carmen should follow the core values of the PAX Universal Center, which she is doing. Her trip to Shasta uplifted her and now she is back in the daily details of the organization. She is a visionary and is sustained by visions.

The PAX Center is based on my ethics of peace, truth, and politically right behavior. She should continue to shine her Light and my concepts to the world — her world — which is so needed. Right thinking. Right guidance.

Peace, Love, and Harmony, Saint Germain.

Saint Germain

From Barbara:

For many, St. Germain is considered a legendary spiritual master of ancient wisdom. He is often said to have been the Count of St.

Germain who lived a very active life (1710-1784), as a composer, inventor, pianist, adventurer, etc. Not long ago, when we were at Mount Shasta visiting a friend, we were surprised to see a recent painting on the wall of a male whose features looked exactly as Saint Germain's features. This one on the wall was dressed in modern-day clothes.

MASAMI SAIONJI

Masami Saionji was born in Tokyo and is descended from the Okinawa Royal Ryukyu family. Her education was extensive and she has lived in Europe and in North America. Throughout her life, she has been traveling extensively to further world peace, and, for that reason, she is the Chairperson of The World Peace Prayer Society, Goi Peace Foundation and Byakko Shinko Kai.

She has been a close follower of the concepts of spiritual leader Masahisa Goi who ardently believed in a peaceful world. After his death, Masami Saionji continued to carry on his ideals. Her world efforts have been recognized, and she is continually called to speak. In 2016 she was given a Barbara Fields Peace Award which honors distinguished women leaders. In 2013, at the United Nations in New York City, we attended as she conducted a ceremony called United for a Culture of Peace.

And, we have met her in Amsterdam, The Netherlands, when we and she attended a ceremony especially concentrating on the theme of peace and reconciliation between the religions of Muslims, Hindus, Buddhists, Jews, and Christians. During our time in Amsterdam, we three were at a ceremony commemorating a new peace pole planted in front of the Peace Palace. A photograph was taken of this ceremony, and it is now on the cover of our book, 2013 and Beyond, Part II. With a group of people, Masami Saionji is kneeling in front of the peace pole, and Margaret and I are on either side of the peace pole.

Several times we have visited and sometimes spoken in Japan. One time, Masami Saionji invited us to be guests of her organization, Byakko Shinko Kai. Hundreds came from all over the world to support the concept of peace that can be achieved by the coming together of different religious beliefs. Her sanctuary is in direct view of the sacred mountain of Mount Fuji.

Emma Kunz

From Barbara:

A few years ago, Margaret and I were traveling to Switzerland to meet Annelis Kessler who works for world peace.

While we were with Annelis Kessler, she suggested we visit the museum and grotto of Emma Kunz. We knew Emma Kunz (1892–1963) once lived in the German-speaking part of Switzerland, and a short drive would take us to her museum and grotto.

The day was warm and friendly as we drove to her place. When we arrived, we learned that the museum was temporarily closed during the noon hour. And so, we waited for the opening at a nearby garden where we examined the plants. About 150 feet from us, we saw a cat slowly coming toward us. This was a brilliantly long-haired white cat, and we watched her moving slowly forward. We had never seen anything quite so beautiful!

Then, when the museum opened, we took our attention off the cat and put it on the museum as a man walked out the door. Margaret asked him if he was the director of the museum and the one who had polio as a young child that Emma Kunz healed with powder. He said yes without slowing his pace, and in a moment he was gone. We knew this powder came from a nearby tall cave.

Now it was time to investigate this tall cave which used to be a Roman quarry. We walked slowly inside it thinking it was a healing place. Emma Kunz's people were offering powder* from the cave and we bought some to bring home.

*See Glossary: AIONA A, Swiss Healing Rock Powder.

————————

From Margaret:

Later, I am channeling artist and healer Emma Kunz. Were you the cat that was coming to see us?

Emma: *Yes.*

Margaret: Barbara and I know your amazing artwork helped people solve personal, psychological problems. It is my understanding that you did not speak during your healing sessions. The analysis work, the solving of the problem, was done by your drawing which you did in front of the patient. This opened the door to clarity and released the problem that was weighing on the mind and spirit of the patient.

Maybe the person was so concentrated on your analysis and resolution of the problem that it was resolved through your pen and pencil strokes. You led the way out of a mental/emotional tangle and allowed the patient to be relieved of the burden. The love you passed on, the desire for resolution, led to creating a healthy relationship with the self and others.

Emma comments: *Patience, Love, Compassion, Diligence, Focus, Effort, Intent set the suffering one free. No words. Just action. Drawing on my part and watching intently on his/her part.*

The pain disappears slowly with the line drawing. The suffering is put on the paper and then released. The person leaves healed.

It works through faith and trust, and the person was not to retrace the mental thoughts that got him or her into that state.

I ask: Other healers are not artists. Is there another way to help?

Emma answers: *Each healer finds his or her own way. That is why the world is so fascinating now. Within the darkness, there is Light.*

Love, expansiveness, infinity frees the soul — like a bird set free from a cage to fly freely and go anywhere. No barriers. No blocks. No sadness. No depression. Only Light. Only Love. Only Peace within the Self.

Love,

Emma

Rudolf Steiner

From Barbara:

Rudolf Steiner (1861-1925) was an Austrian philosopher and social reformer whose active brain had him looking into many, many subjects. He wrote and wrote, and his writing appeared in forty volumes of books, essays, plays, etc. His writings were so stimulating, they led to many reforms, such as reforms in education.

Steiner began a Waldorf Education project that encouraged the use of a child's experience. He emphasized that the whole child, including the heart and mind, must be educated. And he said that a child must be taught to work with the hands as well as with the mind so as to learn to conquer challenges and find solutions as well as learn to be a creative thinker. He must learn science and math and music because his fingers need to become nimble like the mind. A child must learn how to analyze complex concepts which will teach him how to be a critical, creative thinker.

Rudolf Steiner's concept of education was put under the label of Waldorf Education, and these schools are found in various places throughout the world. In New York, a Rudolf Steiner school was formed in 1928 and remains.

CHAPTER 5

Yellowstone

From Barbara:

As I am writing you, today is July 4, 2017, a holiday to celebrate my country's break with Britain. Even though independence was desired a long time ago, today we are friends.

Breaks often mean negativity and negativity can result in Mother Earth being negative. However, during those days, I do not remember reading about Mother Earth's negativity such as earthquakes and volcanic eruptions. But, today we have been experiencing earth rumbles and volcanic activity. Why?

In 2012, Mother Earth experienced what is called a Cosmic Trigger that gave her the ability to ascend to higher dimensions. Now everything on her has the possibility to rise to higher dimensions.

We have been increasingly aware of volcanic action and earthquakes. Are we reaching catastrophic happenings because of the Ascension?

Over the last few years, James Tyberonn, who has access to Masters in the Higher Worlds, has given us information that Mother Earth is adjusting herself to fit into a Higher dimension. Her electromagnetic force is affected and she is trying to balance these energies.

There are certain places on her that have powerful energy, such as Yellowstone. Here is a famous geyser called Old Faithful that explodes on a regular basis.

Millions visit Yellowstone yearly, and one reason is to watch its gem, Old Faithful, exploding on a regular basis. Now we are beginning to realize that earthquakes happening on a regular basis at Yellowstone help in a positive way to send this energy outward.

Apparently, Yellowstone has a very thin crust and just below its surface is molten magma. The spin of the earth plays a part in a natural way to bring balance to the whole planet. The geyser called Old Faithful plays its own part in this.

Yellowstone has nearly half of the world's geysers, also called Hot Springs. Some of them are Riverside Geyser, Steamboat, and Great Fountain. The latter is called Fountain Geyser because of the way the fountain rises. Some geysers shoot straight up, and others shoot sideways.

The geysers at Yellowstone have a unique quality because of evidence in the water of Sulfur and Silicate Quartz. Sulfur has a healing quality, and Silica, in a positive manner, affects the Solar Plexus Chakra to expand consciousness. Some have called the water at Yellowstone the Fountain of Youth because of the water's rejuvenating properties.

But Yellowstone is not the only place that has rejuvenating healing properties. There are fourteen sacred springs around the world with these same properties. James Tyberonn gives these locations.

Mull, Scotland. Chan Chan, Peru. Tumuc-Humac, Brazil. Nagasaki, Japan. Huesca, Spain. Ekaterinbury, Russia (Ural Mountains). Bethlehem, Israel. Yellowstone, Wyoming, U.S.A. Kilimanjaro, Tanzania. Iceland. Kona, Hawaii. Mt. Cook, New Zealand. Great Artesian Basin, Australia. Sri Lanka.

Margaret and I try to visualize these locations when we think about Mother Earth rumbling to try to regulate and balance these energies. We need to help her.

We need to go to nearby Lake Ontario with our minds ready to dispense this energy. We will take with us small pictures of the world's sacred springs, and we will have these pictures in our hands as we are driving to the lake.

It is early, just 7 a.m. and we nearly have the road to ourselves. There is no traffic to slow us because today is a holiday. People will begin their day leisurely. They will not be jumping into their cars and racing to work.

When we arrive at Lake Ontario, we walk on a long pier to reach ducks floating on the water waiting for specks of food to be dropped to them. In our last book, we told you we put a photograph of the Christ into the water here to help with another matter.

The ducks in the water quickly snap up the specks of bread we throw to them and when we finish, they leisurely float away. Now we have the place to ourselves and we are ready to throw in the pictures of sacred springs. When we throw them in, our minds are on sending powerful positive energy around the world.

We know Mother Earth knows what we are doing. Everything has a consciousness. Yes, Mother Earth has a consciousness. She can see everything, feel everything. When mankind is in conflict with each other, this helps give her a stomachache. Some humans fight, have wars continuing for years with no solution.

On a personal level, I have just learned that friendly neighbors have suddenly come in conflict with each other. I am astonished. I live on a street with neighbors who seem quiet and gentle with each other. But, are they quiet and gentle? I am thinking of nine billion people living on Mother Earth. She can feel everything. Wouldn't negativity continually upset her stomach?

Today, we are trying to help her.

———————

When we visited Yellowstone a few years ago, we stopped at a location selling jewelry being made by a Native American woman. I wanted to buy something and I suddenly felt at my shoulder Native American Chief Joseph. He was indicating that I buy a specific stone. This stone was carved with plates looking the same as plates on the back of a turtle. I knew Native Americans consider this continent to be like the plates of a turtle. And so, yes, I understood why Chief Joseph wanted me to buy that particular stone.

I still carry it in my vest and I still feel as if Chief Joseph is with me. He may no longer be living on Mother Earth, but he knows what we must do to help her.

————————

From Margaret:

Barbara and I have learned that earthquakes can be caused by pressure on Earth plates such as the Pacific Plate, the American Plate, the Eurasian Plate, etc. Yellowstone is not on a plate boundary. Yet, she has many earthquakes. We know she is on the thin crust of the planet and this generates energy. But we do not know the quality of this energy.

Then we learn from James Tyberonn* that places like Yellowstone have become a great benevolent portal for Earth to ascend. Yellowstone can energize the planet with the energy she generates.

*See Glossary: James Tyberonn, Earth-Keeper Chronicles.

Hurray! We will help with this ascension. We will take Yellowstone energy to Lake Ontario, one of the largest fresh water lakes in the world. We will give Yellowstone energy to the Great Lakes and then to all the waters of the world.

As we have already mentioned, water has a consciousness. We can connect her energy to all the waters of the world to help with the Ascension.

It is a holiday when we drive to Lake Ontario. As we are approaching, we see a large international regatta forming of Olympic-sized sailboats going out to the lake through the harbor channel. We are near them as they motor out to begin the race in open water.

At the lake, we begin walking to the end of a long pier. Along the way we feed the ducks. People are walking on the pier with their children. All ages are present. Fishermen are fishing on both sides of the pier.

Now I look up and see a rainbow in the sky – a horizontal rainbow– a seal of today. A FIRE RAINBOW. Other people are noticing. All are interested in the rainbow!!! I feel the Masters are with us. We are carrying powerful energy to the lake that will be sent around the world.

We are carrying the sacred springs pictures that Barbara has already mentioned.

When we are at the end of the pier, a fisherman removes his stationary rod so we can move to the center point of the pier facing the lake and the wind. Here, Barbara and I place the tiny sacred spring pictures in the water. We feel great joy and fulfillment! We are under the rainbow.

Slowly we return to the shore and all seems in line for the day. People seem uplifted, joyful. There is a fisherman, a yacht person with binoculars, and a Nepalese family on an outing. Everyone is happy.

Mission accomplished. Our mission of uniting the waters of the world for balance and healing.

AUM.

Earlier, when we are reading about the sacred springs water, we remember Lanto and the Ascended Masters whose focus is at the Grand Tetons near Yellowstone. Lanto helped us on an earlier trip to Yellowstone.

Today we feel he is a part of our trip to Lake Ontario and the energizing of the waters of the world. Lanto carries the Sun within his heart to light the flame in all hearts. I am thinking of healer Braco and I am asking if Lanto and Braco are the same.

Answer: No. Separate. Their messages are the same.

——————

Here is another message, a channeling from Emma.

I say to her, Yellowstone is on our plate again and we have found the world's sacred springs that are connected to Yellowstone. We have focused on all these sacred springs to expand energy throughout the world. Are we also to focus on the Yellowstone geyser called Fountain of Youth?

Emma responds: *It is what your heart calls you to do. Use the Fountain of Youth (Geyser) as a center pole and have the thirteen others spin around it.*

This will bring the energy into Yellowstone and send the energy outwards globally to the waters of the world and their life forms.

Another way would be to have all the springs activated as the jewel crown for Mother Earth.

See how you feel. You have a direct line to Yellowstone and so use it. The connection is not forgotten. It was sealed with a Fire Rainbow.

——————

Now that the sacred springs pictures are in the water, I want to turn my attention to giving the Vortexes to the water.

After I leave the long pier to reach the beach, I walk across the sand to find a clear sandy space near the water. The water is clear and calm as I am ready to give the Vortexes to the water.

I put down my bag, bring out the Vortexes, and begin drawing carefully the twenty-two Vortex Symbols along the beach at the edge of the water. When each pair of Symbols is drawn, I speak the name of the Vortex created and the water responds.

By the time the Spiritual Freedom of Man Symbol is put down, the water is totally engaged taking in the Symbols. It likes the Symbols of Movement and Balance connected to Strength, Health and Happiness. Also, the Symbols of Innocence, Truth and Family connected to the Spiritual Protection of the Family.

Onward I draw as the clear waves take the Symbols so that all the Symbols are taken when I finish.

I feel totally at peace with the lake and all the waters of the planet.

Then I take out the Blessings Chimes and ring them softly for the sound and vibration of the delicate waves coming in as crossed currents.

The sound of the Chimes is in total harmony with the waves, and then I hear an etheric set of Chimes in harmony with the waves.

I ring the Chimes to the water, to Yellowstone, and to all the waters of the world. All are united.

I feel blessed to hear the Angels of a higher frequency.

Yes, a blessed moment!

AUM.

———————

From Barbara:

I need to tell you about one more aspect of Yellowstone. Close by, in the Grand Tetons, is a place called the Royal Teton Retreat for the great White Brotherhood. It is my understanding that every Summer Solstice and every Winter Solstice there is a grand meeting at this place. As humans sleep, they can travel and meet the Masters of ancient times. They will be given wisdom about our planet and what is needed for her.

While Margaret and I are still working on Yellowstone for Mother Earth, we know that Lanto, a great Master, has an etheric retreat in the Tetons Mountain range near Yellowstone. Will he be there?

Just now we are two days from the Winter Solstice and we will check on Lanto's location. He has become a Master of Light, and it is said that the Divine Spark living within him, the three-fold flame, is evident as a golden glow being seen coming through his chest.

Lord Lanto wanted others to have a spark within themselves. Today, centuries after he practiced this, it is being taught by several Masters. One of them is Braco who gives information about having a divine spark. We have written about him in our chapter, Healers and Spiritual Beings. Today's computers will show him freely open to the public for three days. We love to watch him.

———————

From: Margaret:

We have been reviewing the Royal Teton Retreat when the matter of the Winter Solstice comes up, December 21, New York time. During this time, we know there can be resolution and recalibration of important issues.

Because we have been working hard writing the book, I can hardly lift my mind off the text we are writing.

I receive a channeling:

You must pick an issue that is weighing on your soul and present it to the Masters for their wisdom.

You can do it now or in the evening.

I say, my heart is terribly worried about the treatment of the Earth — the Elements of Fire, Water, Land and Air. They are so vital to the continuation of life on this planet.

Answer: *There is a school of thought here on Mother Earth. If one disrespects one aspect of Mother Earth's balance, the other aspects of Mother Earth will come unbalanced.*

Look at the floods in Texas, the hurricanes in the Caribbean, the fires in California. These are occurrences of imbalance.

From these occurrences, humans will learn how to cooperate and work with Nature instead of plundering Nature. The more damage to Mother Earth, the more extreme conditions will occur with the elements.

Land — more earthquakes; Water — more floods and droughts; Air — more storms and hurricanes; Fire — more wild fires.

Come into center in your own heart chamber or our chambers at the Grand Tetons retreat. Act singly. Know great numbers are working. This is the time of uplift to higher dimensions. Always walk in love and kindness.

Observe that the Universal Law of Movement and Balance travels with Spiritual Strength, Health, and Happiness. Find the balance between these two.

With love, your friends from the Higher World here at the Grand Tetons.

CHAPTER **6**

The Pacific

Mount Agung and Vanuatu

From Barbara:

October 16, on the island of Bali in Indonesia, we learned that volcano Mount Agung was experiencing more than 1,000 earthquakes a day. A state of emergency was already in place. Volcano sirens were ready to warn the people of more eruptions and a need to run. There has been worry that earthquakes would activate magma coming upwards from the bowels of the volcano. This could kill many people.

By October, more than 180,000 local residents had run from their homes. About 150,000 went to evacuation camps.

Mount Agung's past brings fear to the people. In 1963, explosions from the mountain killed many. Years ago when I was in Bali, I learned that in 1963 the mountain had such a tremendous eruption, lava poured out and quickly moved across the land destroying it. It stopped at a pagoda-style temple and destroyed everything except two small animal statues. I saw these two small animal statues when I last visited Bali and now I am remembering them.

I am writing to you as if Bali is a dot in the Pacific area. Actually, Bali is Indonesia's top tourist destination with nearly five million visitors coming per year.

At the end of November, Mount Agung erupted and about 59,000 travelers were stranded because 400 flights were cancelled. The governor asked island hotels to allow tourists to stay free of charge.

———————

From Margaret:

At the end of September, I channel asking what we can do to quiet Mount Agung.

Use the Universal Symbol of Movement and Balance, the Whale Symbol, to help stabilize Mother Earth.

Use the Songlines — moving energy — positive frequency.

Make a mandala of day lilies with the flowers facing outwards. Present this as a gift to the volcano.

———————

We print out many elaborate day lilies and combine them with each other. Then we print out a photograph of Mount Agung and we place the day lilies with the Mount Agung photograph.

———————

From Barbara:

We did this on September 29 and there was no eruption, but, as mentioned earlier, Mount Agung increased its earthquakes to more than 1,000 a day.

We realized that peaceful energy needed to be sent to the waters of the Pacific area to calm it. Hopefully, Mount Agung would respond.

To help send peaceful energy, we go to waters near us. With our minds, we expand our thoughts to the Pacific. We drive along Lake

Ontario, part of an enormous waterway of five connected lakes, and we send peaceful thoughts to the Pacific. We know these thoughts are not restricted by physical distance.

We know the world is on edge. We feel the entities within the Pacific framework are on edge. The Pacific is so upset!

————————

From Margaret:

I channel to the Brothers and Sisters connected to the Pacific and I am told:

Create a point of peace and spread it outwards. Use the energy field of the Niagara Escarpment, the glistening waters, shimmering Light, solid rock layers.

Also, create a force field from the Sacred Lake in the Adirondacks to Sodus Point and then to Sea Breeze, to Niagara Falls.

————————

More channeling:

Call on the Brothers and Sisters of the Higher Worlds to join in imprinting this peace frequency over the Pacific.

Create a cup of mountain energies – Mount Shasta, Denali, Chugash Mountains to Mount Fuji, to Kilauea to Mauna Loa to Mauna Kea. Include Mount Kailash, Uluru, Bromo. Place their strength, their positive energy over the Pacific and the world.

Bring the Sun Discs in as well. These are Balance Points across the world.

Ask the Elemental entities to step in to assist. Land — the crystals. Water — the dolphins and whales. Air — the clouds, the angels. Fire— the Sun and the core of Mother Earth.

The Elementals have a resonance, a frequency that harmonizes and expands when joined together.

Humans need to join to work with the Elementals to stabilize the planet.

Love and Gratitude spread peace. Humanity needs to turn down the separateness and speak to the whole.

Focus on the whole and blur the parts – Universal Land, Universal Water, Universal Air, Universal Fire. The Elements have no boundaries.

Spread the frequency of peace. Expand peace consciousness through the Niagara Escarpment points and the created energy cup of the mountains.

With Love from your Brothers and Sisters of the Oceans and all of us.

––––––––––

Barbara sends a message to the Global Meditations Network:

Hello from my heart, everyone, this is Barbara Wolf.
Global Meditations Network.
http://www.globalmeditations.com

You are being asked to use your mind to calm a potential for a big volcanic explosion at Mount Agung on the island of Bali in the Pacific.

Please hold in your minds Peace, Love, and Light for this problem.

Barbara Wolf

––––––––––

December 8, Mount Agung began spewing out grey plums thousands of feet into the air. Indonesian authorities issued a state of alert that was the highest alert ever.

With a drone, authorities were able to look into the volcano and they did not see a red glow, which was a relief.

When ash was pouring out of the crater in November, this was called cold lava. It was pouring out rather than erupting, which meant there was not enough pressure coming from the volcano to cause an explosion, an eruption.

The lava tended to be thick and sticky, and it did not flow away but tended to pile up thick near the vent. Nevertheless, what was happening created a caution for all who live there. People remain fearful.

————————

More from Barbara:

In October, Vanuatu Island in the Pacific started having a problem. Smoke began pouring upward from the middle of the island. All the people, about 10,000, were being evacuated. Every boat, large and small, took them out of there. They had to leave everything behind them including their animals. One woman said she was worried about leaving her animals which included a pig and three cows.

When I think of the plight of animals living in Vanuatu, I write to Chief Golden Light Eagle, head Native American who is ready to present ceremonies during the Full Moon of the Bear.

I know it is believed that bear energy can open gates that have been closed. Also, the bear is able to help heal the minds of the people. This is called Bear Medicine.

I think about the helpless animals in Vanuatu, such as the three cows and one pig, and I also think of all the animals of the Pacific and all the animals of the world.

During Chief Golden Light Eagle's ceremony for the Full Moon of the Bear, I want him to know about Vanuatu and other areas where there are trapped animals.

Yes, I think the Bear Medicine that Chief Golden Light Eagle can send out during the Native American ceremonies can be a help.

———————

I am not an expert on volcanoes and earthquakes and what makes them cause eruption. Obviously it has to do with energy lines. In 2011, the Pacific island of Vanuatu strongly exploded with a big earthquake. It is suspected that this earthquake triggered an even larger earthquake to the north, in the Pacific facing a Japanese nuclear power plant complex located on the coast. The Japan earthquake was a 9.1 which produced a huge tsunami that raced to the coast overcoming and breaking three nuclear reactors.

To this day authorities have not been able to contain the nuclear material still continuing to go into the Pacific. This remains a danger not only for the people of Japan, but for all the living fish and animals that have the Pacific as their home.

In an earlier book to you, we have mentioned this.

———————

We want Peace, Love, and Light to calm the Pacific as well as all of Mother Earth. We want her to be full of Joy and full of love.

We want Joy and Love for the Pacific.

———————

From Barbara:

Throughout September, October and November, we have worked to calm Mount Agung. When the end of November arrived, we continued our efforts, even though we knew that Mount Agung had erupted.

We do not want our efforts to be considered a failure.

Yes, we will continue giving Mother Earth Peace, Love, and Light until all Peace is achieved.

CHAPTER 7

Korea

From Barbara:

A great shock! September 15, we learn that North Korea has tested a ballistic missile that flew over their neighbor Japan and landed in the Pacific.

We have close friends in Japan and we quickly learn that the Japanese have been worried about the testing of nuclear weapons by North Korea. Apparently, North Korea has recently tested six. We also learn the mountain used for testing is so powerful, if the mountain explodes, destruction would be terrifying.

In 1950, when war began between North and South Korea, I was young and growing up and other matters dominated my attention. Well, this past September a check of the Internet said that at least 2.5 million people died. The fighting went on and on until finally the United Nations found a way for the warriors to accept a truce that remains. The front line at the time of the truce was accepted as a boundary between North and South Korea, and it is a boundary today. There has never been a final peace treaty.

After this year's missile launch, peace worker James Twyman called for a Worldwide Synchronized Meditation for the Korean Peninsula.* It would be September 16, 12 noon, New York time, and he would position himself at the border of North and South Korea. He asked everyone throughout the world to join this peace meditation.

*See Glossary: James Twyman meditation.

Well, no one expected that the weather would interfere with Twyman's plans. However, hurricanes causing record damage were roaring north toward the United States. Just south, James Twyman was in Cuba helping to promote peace. Almost immediately, Hurricane Irma came down hard on Cuba and we were worried about him. But he was able to survive.

Then, when he learned it would be too dangerous for him to be at the border between North and South Korea for the meditation, plans needed to be changed. But the meditation was not cancelled. Twyman would be at his home in the U.S.A. with others joining him by phone. His line could take a conference call of about 500.

He emailed everyone to join him by phoning at the beginning of the meditation.

––––––––––––

From Margaret:

Of interest to us is that during today's dark period of growing conflict between nations, we learn about the Unicorns. Why have we learned this now?

I ask Emma and she says:

You are reacting to fear and aggression which means no Light. The Unicorn appears to give Light. There have always been Unicorns in North Korea. The land has felt their Light. People hold the legacy of Unicorn in their psyche.

Call on the frequency of the Unicorn to appear in everyone's heart. When the heart is full of Light, it feels and receives Love and gives out Light.

Place Light on North Korea. Honor the presence of the Unicorn which softens the heart and turns one to Purity, Wisdom and Compassion. This changes the frequency of this thinking of happenings on the planet now.

With love form Emma and the Unicorns.

———————————

From Barbara:

The Internet tells us that the Koreans have known a long time about Unicorns. Also, we find Unicorn references in Chinese and Japanese mythology. Some Western literature speaks about the Unicorns.

These are gentle and beneficial creatures, and they only become angry and fierce when the atmosphere of innocence becomes threatened.

I write to James Twyman saying that the Unicorn has made its home in North Korea for a great number of years. These silent ones feel today's tension. We welcome your concentration on Korea and we know great numbers of people as well as the Unicorns will be focusing on your September 16 prayers and meditation.

Remember when you were on the Golan Heights. After your magnificent peace presentation, the wolves howled. The Unicorns do not howl but they will be silently cheering your efforts.

Best regards from all who appreciate your great efforts to help the world.

———————————

Also from Barbara:

It is early morning in North Korea and the hearts of the people are rested and relaxed as we help the Unicorns, great numbers of them, send White Light to the North Koreans to change their attitudes from negative to positive.

But also we help send the White Light of the Unicorns to the South Koreans, Japanese, Chinese, Russians, Americans—all who are involved with the desperate need to settle Korean differences that have built to catastrophic proportions.

We play specific music that has a powerful reed sound, and because we have successfully used it before, that is why I feel the Unicorns will respond to help solve the problem.

I ask the Hierarchy if our technique is helpful and they say *Yes.*

_____

From Margaret:

In meditation, I visualize I am at a waterfall in a dense forest and I call in the Unicorns. I feel their presence and one slightly touches me. I ask for PEACE and I know they hear my request of focusing on Light for the people.

I want the frequency of the Unicorns to shine their Light on the leaders of Korea, Japan, United States, China, and Russia—to put Light into the hearts of the people to see peace instead of war confrontation.

I know the Earth is like a ship on rough seas and all on board need to cooperate in order to not sink the Ship of Life. I hold the Unicorn frequencies in my heart and I let go of fear that tends to spiral in my mind.

I feel the High Frequencies of the Unicorns dancing in the presence of the mystic waterfalls. I feel the Openness, Stillness, Peace. The Unicorns and waterfalls open the hearts of the people to fill them with Light.

The Light of the Unicorn returns.

_____

Later, we speak with a friend in Japan who says everyone is extremely worried about North Korea and Japan. We continue our concentration on the problem, and we play the Ode to Joy music that has 10,000 Japanese people singing together.* Yes, togetherness. That is important.

*See Glossary: Beethoven, Ode to Joy.

We eat at a nearby Japanese Restaurant, and on entering the restaurant, we feel as if we are in Japan. The food is delicious. The staff is very kind and attentive. We send our love energies to Japan.

The weather has become perfect. Bright sunshine and only a hint of clouds. A moderate breeze and favorable, warm temperatures. Perfect, perfect, perfect. We keep our minds on the perfection of weather and loving thoughts to Japan as well as to Korea.

I know we must continue receiving help from the Higher Worlds.

They say: *The door is open. We are available.*

————————

From Barbara:

Yes, I know we must continue meditating for Peace in North Korea. We can use relaxing, meditation music "Flower Canyon" by Tim Janis. (He is mentioned in the Glossary, Chapter 2.)

————————

From Margaret:

In meditation, I hold the white quartz crystal from France, the shell from Australia, and the rock from Broken Hill, Australia. These can all expand Light and Sound frequencies.

First we give Peace to the countries in conflict—to blanket the frequency of the land and the environment. Peace in the country, peace in society, peace in community, peace in the family, peace throughout.

Then we give Love to fill the hearts of the people so they feel joy and harmony and peace. All are given Love. No one is left out.

Then, the White Light is given for healing and for the frequency of Joy, Love, and Peace.

Now we concentrate on White Light, Pure Light, and I feel the presence of the Angels. I can also feel the closeness of the Masters. I call out to the Dolphins and Whales to join in.

The music swells and the heart opens.

Peace, Love and Light are sent out across the world.

May Peace Prevail on Earth.

AUM.

――――――――

I say to Saint Germain, we are concerned about North Korea testing a nuclear device. We are worried and the Japanese people are worried. We have put peace frequencies over Japan and North and South Korea. Can you give advice?

Saint Germain responds: *Hold your intention steady.*

May Peace Prevail On Earth.

Hold it down and connect it to Mother Earth's heart. Call in the Angels for protection to guard humanity and life forms on the planet.

May Peace Prevail On Earth in every square inch. The planet has a mighty force field. Link into all the inches of peace and spread it all over the planet.

May Peace Prevail On Earth.

Designate your area as a peace zone—where you sleep, where you eat, where you work. Spread this peace zone out across the world.

Hold it in place by Love.

Send it out by Love and Light.

Peace, Love and Light.

May Peace Prevail On Earth.

————————

From Barbara:

I hear the soft humming of the Unicorns as they respond to the powerful music of Love that we are playing for them as they work to open the hearts of the people to the positive.

I do not know how many Unicorns are working but there are hundreds. They are sending White Light for the desperate need to settle differences that have been built to catastrophic proportions.

We play specific music that has a powerful reed sound. We have successfully used it before and I feel the Unicorns will successfully respond to the problem.

I ask the Higher World if our technique is helpful and they say yes. They also say, *we would not have you do your way of thinking, of working, if you would not be successful. You do not have to go out to count the nickels and dimes. Continue, continue, continue with the work.*

————————

Also from Barbara:

Here are notes about Korea:

A few years ago, if I wanted to fly from the U.S.A. to the Far East, Los Angeles always had planes to Seoul, South Korea that would go here and there in the Far East. From time to time, I would go to Hong Kong via that route. I found Hong Kong to be fun, and I liked taking the tram to the top of Victoria Peak. This was easy enough to do, and the view at the top was spectacular!

August 1996, when I was flying from Hong Kong on my way home, I was sitting next to a talkative Korean woman who spoke awful English. She told me in her awful English that she had paid 800 U.S. dollars to learn it, and now I am her chance to speak it!

Well, I listened and listened as she stumbled along and I could hardly understand a word. Finally, I put on my earphones to listen to music, but she had more to say to me. She pulled off my earphones and continued to speak. Oh!

This was in 1996. By now, I hope her English has improved.

———————

I want to tell you another experience in 1996 at the Seoul, South Korean airport. Here, I meet an American military service man who had just finished his duty in Korea. He was stationed near the DMZ, the meeting place of North and South Korea. Now he was returning home to Pennsylvania to be with his wife and three children before being transferred to Kentucky.

I knew that Korea had been hit by floods and I asked him if he had been affected. Yes. For one week, he replied, he and his buddies had been stranded in a barracks without light or running water.

I asked him how he liked his Korean duty and he looked at me without replying.

———————

From Margaret:

Here are my notes about Pat and Frank Hunt,* my aunt and uncle who worked in Korea helping the refugees after the 1953 stopping of the Korean War.

*See Glossary: See Pat and Frank Hunt Korean refugee work.

They traveled to Kunsan, a southwest fishing port in South Korea to work with 15,000 refugees who were North Korean widows, children, and elderly that had fled from the fighting. The refugees were housed in a temporary camp of tents and make-shift hovels without heating or running water. The camp had off-and-on electricity.

Beside helping the refugees, also needed was the rebuilding of a hospital that had been bombed and became an informal refugee camp. Families camped by the beds of the sick. The United Nations asked the American Friend Service Committee and the British Friends to send staff because almost all the former staff had fled during the war. One doctor came once a week to distribute medicine if available. Doctors, nurses and relief workers were needed.

My Uncle Frank worked on the reconstruction of the hospital as well as the establishing of a tuberculosis ward, a training program for local nurses, and the treating of critically ill people. To help with this project, three doctors came, six nurses came, and seven experienced relief workers came to help with this project.

My Aunt Pat worked to provide bedding, clothing, educational supplies and self-help activities. She organized the making of local food and the raising of chickens. To provide dignity and comfort for the families, women were provided with rolls of cloth to make Korean-style cloths. Donated peddle sewing machines were used.

In the United States every Quaker Meeting had a mitten tree for Korean refugees. Soon after the beginning of the year and at the time of heavy snows, big containers of bright colored mittens arrived for the children. These were unloaded in the warehouse where the women's sewing work was done. Each mother helped her children pick out their favorite colored mittens. To everyone's delight, the children then ran out in the snow and wildly threw snowballs. My aunt said the children could finally play in the snow because their little hands were protected.

I had such admiration for my Aunt Pat and Uncle Frank. They were indeed my role model for service to humanity. Aunt Pat also taught my sister and me how to eat with chopsticks, and we enjoyed using them while eating and remembering Pat and Frank's work in Korea.

CHAPTER 8

United Arab Emirates And India

From Barbara:

Margaret and I have been invited as speakers for the 18th International Conference of Chief Justices of the World to be held at City Montessori School in Lucknow, India, November 10 through 14.

Over the years, Dr. Jagdish Gandhi, head of the school, has invited us and we have attended several times. It is fun to go even though it is difficult to reach Lucknow because it is so far away.

This year we begin our journey by stopping a short time at the United Arab Emirates to visit our friend Salwa Zeidan. Then we fly to Bombay, now called Mumbai, where we transfer to another plane taking us to Lucknow and the conference.

But first I need to tell you about our trip to Abu Dhabi in the Emirates. November 3, we fly to New York City where we transfer to an Etihad flight. This airline, if you choose certain dates, will give you a very reasonable flight to Abu Dhabi, and then you can catch another flight to wherever you are going in that area, such as India.

In any case, Margaret and I take a quick flight to New York City where we transfer to an Etihad flight taking us non-stop to Abu Dhabi. This is a LONG flight, but the plane is comfortable and most of the passengers begin sleeping practically non-stop. The stewardesses are pleasant and accommodating and quickly fulfill whatever tasks are required in the hushed cabin.

There is no need to look out the windows because the flight is during dark hours. Because there are no bumps, the pilot does not have to put on warning signals for his passengers. When we reach Abu Dhabi, it is daylight.

We exit the plane and enter the terminal building which is a big one, full of activity. There is no delay collecting our baggage, and inspection of our passports is quick.

Soon we are outside the terminal building and inside the car of Salwa Zeiden's husband who has come to the airport to meet us and take us to his family home where we will stay for a couple days.

We have told Salwa our desire to visit what I consider the biggest mosque in the world, and it is prominently located in Abu Dhabi. We know that seeing Sheikh Zayed Grand Mosque* will be overwhelming! It has an awesome collection of immense white marble domes, and the mosque complex itself has a capacity for holding 41,000 or more worshipers.

*See Glossary: Sheikh Zayed Grand Mosque, Abu Dhabi.

Yes, Margaret and I do want to see this mosque. Over the years we have watched it grow, but now that it is finished, WOW, we want to see it!

Salwa cannot join us because she is extremely busy helping to set up paintings at a big art show that will soon open to the public.

Her driver takes us to the Sheikh Zayed Grand Mosque and tells us to phone when we are ready to leave the mosque. We do not have cellphones with us, but we are told this does not matter. Because everyone has a cellphone, we only need to ask anyone to phone for us.

With that thought in mind, we are dropped off at the mosque and we are given long gowns to wear before following many, many who have come for the same reason we are here—to visit the biggest and best mosque in the world.

We are not of the mosque's faith, but the mosque is open to everyone who wants to visit. We amble along with hoards of visitors as we reach big pools of water outside the mosque. When we come to a place where we need to leave our shoes before entering the interior of the mosque, we choose to leave them where we hope they will be waiting for us when we return for them.

Well, we do have a moment or two of anxiety when we return to where we thought we left our shoes and they are not there! A helpful mosque guide takes us to another shoe place and our shoes are not among the many, many, many shoes.

Help!

But then we find another collection of shoes, and yes, our shoes are there!

In any case, seeing the mosque has been wonderful. When our feet are ready to stop walking, we ask a security guard to phone Salwa's driver. The security guard immediately uses his cellphone, and within minutes, we are picked up.

Now, I need to tell you about the art show Salwa has been helping to prepare. She has arranged for us to receive temporary passes to enter, and we are amazed at the huge extent of the exhibit. First, Salwa, who has owned galleries for many years, takes us to the area where the art of her particular artists is being displayed. And then she guides us through the entire building of art displays.

We are a couple days too early for the opening of the big exhibit, but after we return home from our India talks, we phone Salwa and she tells us the exhibit has been a great success. In fact, all the paintings have been sold that she has displayed for her artists!

INDIA

Now it is time to explain about our journey to India. We have been invited to attend and speak at the 18th International Conference of Chief Justices of the World. From Abu Dhabi, we first fly to Mumbai to catch a plane to Lucknow. By the way, Mumbai was earlier called Bombay, and the word Bombay, when we were traveling, was often used.

In any case, at the Mumbai airport, we wait nine hours for our next flight to Lucknow. But this Mumbai airport is QUITE SOMETHING! It is HUGE, and its mind-boggling interior has exquisite architecture and features.

It is called the Chhatrapati Shivaji International Airport, and it is the second busiest airport in India. We sit and watch lines of fifty plus people waiting to board a plane. When one plane is filled with passengers and on its way, another line of 50 plus passengers will be waiting to board the next plane. This process goes on and on and on.

We sit and watch, and then, just before our flight to Lucknow is ready to be boarded, we meet Divino Roberto Verissimo of Brazil who will be with us at the conference in Lucknow. He, too, will be speaking.

Our flight is short and when we arrive at Lucknow, a dear friend has arranged for someone to pick us up at the airport and take us to the City Montessori School. This is the largest school in the world and the site of the yearly Chief Justice conference. Here, we are given a comfortable guest room which overlooks a big, beautiful water garden for people to sit to eat meals while they are attending the conference.

When we arrive, we have the water garden to ourselves and Divino Roberto Verissimo. The chief justice people are sightseeing outside Lucknow. Our interest is not sightseeing with them because we have visited sightseeing places during earlier conferences.

But yes, we three will be sightseeing together before the conference begins. Our intention is to visit hospitals. Two years ago, Margaret and I were taken out of the city where we encountered rural people having a problem we tried to solve. And we did solve it. In a couple days, my talk at the conference will involve this 'out of the city' encounter, because it involves creating a culture of unity and peace, which is this year's conference theme.

Here is my talk for this year.

Hello from my heart everyone, this is Barbara Wolf.

Today, I want to talk to you about Peace Education and Cross Cultural Understanding.

I am happy, students, that you in your classrooms, are being given an education that emphasizes the great need for peace on our planet.

I have long ago finished with my classroom education, but I have not ended my education. I have become a teacher of myself.

Let me explain.

I live on the North American continent in the country called the United States of America. Nearly every year I connect India to my country by attending a conference being held at your Lucknow school. Usually I listen and sometimes I speak.

India is a big, big country. When I come to Lucknow, I try to understand more of your culture by visiting more of India.

A couple years ago, with a friend, I attended a quick gathering of Indian farmers who planted their crops in big, big fields. The fields were so big, it was impossible to successfully harvest the crops when they were ripe. The only successful harvest was to have professional harvesters with big and expensive machines come to the fields and quickly harvest the ripe crops.

Yes, the crops were successfully harvested, but, the crop money went into the pockets of the harvesters and not into the pockets of the farmers who remained poor and without hope.

However, this dilemma brought a thought to our minds and we suggested to the group that a second profession needed to be tried.

Did the group have a sewing machine? Yes. One machine.

Did the group have a motorcycle? Yes. Two motorcycles.

GOOD!

We suggested that because all women wear the same type of underclothing, the group could sew women's underclothing and then use a motorcycle to take this finished product to a place along the road where the underclothing could be displayed and sold.

And yes, the group accepted the idea, and the next year, when we returned to India, we learned that the idea had been successful! We also learned that some of the profits were used to begin a small pharmacy to sell needs to ill people.

I have added the following to the end of my talk.

This year, I investigated the hospitals in Lucknow to learn about medical care for teeth problems, eye care, immunization, free medicine, and much more.

Students, your minds are big and expansive. You can use them to create your own way to help those who are less fortunate. This will peacefully help your culture.

And yes, we have visited hospitals before the conference begins and I have given my talk. Shishir Srivastava, Head of International Relations at the school and a very good friend, has arranged for a private driver to take us wherever we desired. We told this driver we specifically wanted to visit hospitals, and because we did not know the names of Lucknow hospitals, we wanted the driver to take us where he thought we should go.

And so, we three, Margaret, Divino Roberto and I, plus an interpreter, seated ourselves in the car, relaxed, and allowed the driver to go where he chose. He started out smartly with a couple warning peep-peeps of his horn, and we were soon on our way taking a road packed with other cars going here and there. Of course I am used to being in U.S.A. traffic following the custom of what the British would call driving on 'the wrong side of the road'. Indian drivers are accustomed to driving on the British 'right side of the road'. My view of all this brought tension to my mind.

Twenty years ago, or a bit more, when I first experienced India traffic, it was relatively light. Well, not today! There are hoards of fast-moving motorcycles whose drivers are usually accompanied by 'back seat' riders wearing faces expressing anxiety, as if they are hanging on for dear life!

And there are small, three-wheeled, hooded taxis put-putting along by drivers whose customers are squashed into a seat behind the drivers. Also, there are trucks of different sizes. And there are cars--MANY-- of all sizes and models.

I note there are no stoplights to bring to a halt cars turning in front of drivers. Turning left, right, and sometimes circling.

Our driver moves along smartly with his hand on the horn to do light peep-peeps for cars on all sides of us. Everyone drives with his hand on the horn doing light peep-peeps. No loud peep-peeps expressing impatience. There is no impatience. Everyone knows the road is not normal and everyone knows the drivers are not normal. Every second the cars on the road are swerving left, right, going here and there, turning, crossing in front of oncoming traffic, etc.

I note this is customary, and a bit of impatience is not expressed. I think everyone's mind is hooked exactly to every other mind on the road, and so, everything 'is known' about what everyone will do.

Later, when I return home and am being driven by a taxi driver, a large truck in front of us suddenly turns and my taxi driver blasts with his horn. Impatience—yes.

Well, that taxi driver would have a nervous breakdown driving in India.

In any case, our India driver delivers us to a Lucknow hospital and we wait in the car while he runs into the hospital to announce that foreign visitors have come to see the hospital. He returns with a hospital official and we are soon out of the car and on our way inside the building which I note is packed with people.

Why are there so many people? Certainly all do not seem to be ill. Maybe whole families come with an ailing family member.

Just inside the hospital entrance, we start walking down a crowded corridor and we immediately begin passing small rooms crowded with patiently waiting people. Are they waiting for a family member to meet a hospital official?

We walk past other open-door small rooms and we see the same.

Then our hospital official stops at a small, dark room and asks us to enter. A smiling nurse quietly greets us and we are told that we have entered a room of mothers with freshly delivered babies. In fact, we are told one mother's baby was born thirty-five minutes before we entered.

There are six beds and all are occupied. We visitors quietly put our palms together at our chests to greet them and they smile at us.

I ask the nurse where are the new-born babies, and she, with a slight touch of her hand, flips over the edge of a blanket to reveal a new-born child fast asleep beside its mother.

The mothers are not wearing hospital clothes. It is as if they have given birth at home. In fact, we do not see any patients wearing hospital clothes. I cannot imagine how many hospital clothes would need to be laundered daily if all patients wore them.

Just now I am remembering that at the entrance grounds, about fifty feet from the hospital itself, we passed an elderly man whose body was sunk to the ground with no energy. How could he have come this far on his feet? Maybe someone brought him by bicycle or motorcycle and dropped him off. I know life is not easy for many here in India.

Of the three hospitals we visited in Lucknow, I learn that one of them expects close to 5,000 people coming each day and 3,500 leaving each day.

Think of the PAPER WORK and the FEEDING of so many who come to the hospitals! Actually, we did not see anyone eating in the hospitals, but we did see one big kettle being used to accommodate soup.

————————

Our last stop is at the Sahara Hospital, and this hospital looks well-built and appears to be new. We enter a large, exclusive greeting room with a statue of Goddess Bharatmata guarded by the statues of four fierce lions. My thought is that the goddess is not only guarded by the lions, but they also guard from negativity those who enter the room. Did the guarding include guarding against the negativity of ill health?

A hospital attendant guides us through the hospital, and we note that doors are closed and there are signs on the doors indicating the type of medical afflictions being treated.

We walk along without stopping at these doors until we reach a sign saying this is a restricted area. A door is open and we look in and see a frail woman seated alone wearing her ordinary clothes. Nearby are three women whose faces indicate concern for their ailing friend. They are wearing traditional black robes of Muslim women, and their headgear, which ordinarily would be tightly fastened to hide their faces, is pushed back, revealing their faces.

Our friend, Divino Roberto, when he looks into this room and sees the ailing woman, quickly steps into the room. With his mind fixed on the ailing woman, he passes her three friends without looking at them and takes the ailing woman into his arms. The three women raise their hands to their heads to protect their features, but then they simultaneously realize here is no need to protect their features from Divino Roberto because they know he is not looking at them. They put down their hands.

I stand in the doorway watching Divino Roberto and I know he is sending a full package of Love/Healing to the woman as he firmly embraces her.

Yes, I know he is a healer, and I know the ailing woman and her three friends have realized this. When Divino Roberto has given his energy to the woman and stepped back, his face full of concern for her, I put my hands together and bow in tribute to the ailing woman. Then we leave the room to continue seeing the contents of the hospital.

I walk beside Divino Roberto and make a brief but deep comment— the woman is facing death. Without speaking, he nods in agreement.

The experience of the three hospitals will always be memorable and we know our computers at home will be waiting for us to see hospital photographs sent to us. One of them will be a photograph of Sahara Hospital Administrator Aman Singh Chaudhary standing with us as we three are smiling, smiling, smiling.

Chaudhary, we note when we first encounter him, is a busy, busy man, and his expression when he first meets us is one of patience, similar to what one would expect on the highway when drivers are forced to be patient with traffic. Chaudhary orders tea for us as well as some for himself, plus a well-designed platter of fruit. In a relaxed manner, we drink tea and munch from the fruit platter and smile at him as we ask him questions about the hospital. He politely answers them.

When it is time for photographs to be taken with him, we are smiling at each other and enjoying each other's company. And yes, when we return to our home-bound computers, the photograph he emailed to us shows all of us, including him, smiling and looking happy.

——————————

Before the beginning of the Chief Justice conference, our driver takes us to the Gomti River which runs through Lucknow. It is not difficult to reach. A couple of years ago we sat at the shore listening to about thirty chanters sending energy to the river. This was exactly what we intended to do and we thought it was unusual for such a coincidental happening. In effect, we joined their efforts—we on one side of the river and they on the other side.

Earlier, the river was experiencing vast pollution. And earlier, as we were sending energy, I noted there were few birds drinking the water. That night when we were having supper at Shishir's house, we saw that his apartment overlooked the river. We gave him powerful energy Vortexes to place on his balcony overlooking the river. Later, he emailed saying the government had decided to begin cleaning up the river. This year we wanted to see the progress of the cleanup, and so we went to the shore to make an assessment. Well, we saw no birds, and we felt that drinking the water was still hazardous for them. In my opinion, the Gomti River has a long way to go before birds and animals can safely drink the water.

Interesting, this year our guest rooms, as well as other guest rooms, are supplied with packaged, safe drinking water at no charge to the guests.

——————————

The Chief Justices have been sightseeing and now they, almost 200 of them, arrive at the City Montessori School. Margaret and I watch for their arrival. We are on the second floor near steep steps that lead to a long walkway where students with musical instruments are waiting for the Chief Justices. When they arrive, the students will powerfully play their instruments as a sign of WELCOME.

Unexpectedly, two chairs are brought for us to sit on and watch. At the moment, we are watching the students resting with their instruments as they are strung along the walkway below us. Then, two students who are at the top of the stairs near us begin to walk down the steep stairway. "Hello", they softly say as they pass us. We put out our hands to greet them and they softly take our hands as they begin down the stairs.

Then comes a bit of surprise. Students begin climbing the stairs and when they reach us, they say, "Good morning" and lightly put out their hands. "Hello, hello", we tell them as we take their hands.

The news has quickly spread! The two foreign women will shake hands! Yes, of course. And yes, many students climb up and climb down the stairs. We shake hands with all of them. FUN!

Now the Chief Justices arrive and the students eagerly begin playing their instruments. Large wreaths of orange garlands are around the necks of the Chief Justices. They walk until they reach the stairs of the big auditorium. Then they seat themselves on the steps. Margaret and I are asked to join them and garlands are placed around our necks. Photographs are ready to be taken. Interesting, several years ago one of the day's photographs found its way to a big school wall. It is still hanging. I walk past this photograph and see myself prominently displayed.

After the photographing, we take seats inside the auditorium, which happens to be one of the biggest auditoriums in that part of India. We watch school children perform a United Nations meeting, and I note that the school children are so professional and well rehearsed, it is as if I am looking at a real United Nations meeting.

The purpose of a United Nations performance is to emphasize the reason for the Chief Justices from across world being invited to India. It is to emphasize Article 51 of the Constitution of India which states that the Constitution urges a need to promote international peace and security, to maintain just and honorable relations between nations, to foster respect for international law, and to encourage settlement of international disputes by arbitration.

And yes, it is expected that the nearly 200 Chief Justices who have come to India will follow closely the intentions of Article 51.

My talk on Peace Education and Cross Cultural Understanding, which I have given to you several pages ago, was given the day after the Chief Justices finished their sightseeing and are at the City Montessori School.

Two days later, Margaret has given her talk, and the next day we say good-bye to the Chief Justices and to the City Montessori School children. Now we begin our long trip back to the U.S.A.

But, before writing about our return trip, I need to add one more interesting incident at the Chief Justice meeting. The back of the big auditorium has a lounge where people can sit and relax. When I decided to relax, I entered the lounge area and realized most chairs were occupied by loungers. One chair was vacant and I sat on it.

Nearby, an African Chief Justice was relaxing. After a few moments, for one reason or another, we started a small conversation. I asked him where was his home and he said South Africa. I have visited his homeland only a couple times, and I tell him where I went. He eagerly replied to my comments. I asked if he had visited my homeland and he answered yes, New York City. Then he added he was enrolled in a big New York marathon. Because so many would be enrolled, one has to enroll in a specific time period.

His comments began a revealing of his many trips around the world where he entered marathons. Did he win, I asked? Not always, but sometimes.

WOW!

I am talking to Chief Justice Boissie Mbha.

The reason why I have added this to the India trip chapter is that just as Chief Justice Boisse Mbha is telling me about being from South Africa, which is next door to the country of Zimbabwe, for the first time in many, many years, Zimbabwe is now encountering a very great problem. Its leader, 93-year-old President Robert Mugabe, who has been in charge of Zimbabwe since the 1980's, is under careful scrutiny by the country's military who want him to resign. Words coming from the military say that everything needs to be organized in a non-violent way. Well, often what needs to be organized in a non-violent way turns to violence.

Violence can easily spread. The next-door neighbor of Zimbabwe, South Africa, can easily pick up the baton. I did not speak about this to Chief Justice Boisse Mbha of South Africa, but I started worrying.

Peace is what is needed. Peace, peace, and peace in this currently unstable world.

———————————

It is now November 20 and news about the problem in Africa has been reaching the world's news media. President Robert Mugabe has not resigned. A bank near me has a director from South Africa, and today Margaret and I have visited him to ask about Zimbabwe. He says the country is poor, poor, poor. It used to be a big, thriving farming country, but over the years the land has been taken from the people and farming has dwindled. The people are very, very poor.

He says Robert Mugabe is a millionaire and continues to be wealthy. He has a big, expensive building complex in Hong Kong and expensive enterprises in other places in the world.

November 21, we learn that Robert Mugabe has resigned and we have heard of no violence pertaining to this action.

Margaret and I continued sending healing love energy to Zimbabwe. We did not want the continent of Africa to become unsteady.

CHAPTER 9

United Arab Emirates And India

From Margaret:

November 3:

I am up early with my thoughts on the United Arab Emirates and India trip. We will have eight different flights on this journey and the first one will be JetBlue going to New York JFK Airport.

At JFK Airport, I meet Vernell Crumpter from Florida who is visiting her niece in Abu Dhabi which is where I am first going. We sit together and talk about hurricanes and travel and what to do in Abu Dhabi.

When our plane arrives, we board and wait for the plane to lift off which is smooth. The flight is very long, and so to pass the time, I watch documentaries on the plane's video. The seating is comfortable and there is plenty of legroom.

In the nearby galley area, I enjoy the abstract patterns of lights in the ceiling and reflections on the floor. The stewards and stewardesses are pleasant and helpful.

———————

November 4:

We arrive midday in Abu Dhabi. Two young men assist us through passport control and take us outside to our host, Maurice, husband of our friend Salwa Zeidan. He drives us to their home where our bags are taken upstairs to a front room that has a full set of beautiful paintings of the word of Allah written in calligraphy. From the window, we see a lovely garden.

At lunch we have a delicious salad prepared by Salwa who tells us about the Abu Dhabi Art Fair that will open November 8 and run until November 11.

In the evening, I go to bed early. However, I am up before midnight because I feel I have not landed. I am still in transit. To balance myself, I draw a sailboat with a tall mast representing High Principles and a deep keel representing balance and stability.

I then connect to the crystals of the desert sand here. I must check the origin of the sand crystals. Are they from underwater sea life or ancient fossils or crystalline stones?

I send out Light, Love and Peace to the entire region.

Now I sleep.
————————

November 5:

I wake and delight in watching two baby rabbits enjoying eating and playing in the grass below me. Birds are singing. Salwa gives us a delicious breakfast of pomegranates, yogurt, olives, and other tasty items.

At 10:30 a.m. we go to Abu Dhabi's Sheikh Zayed Grand Mosque, a vast and exquisite building that took twelve years to complete. I see it is full of Light.

Over the years, we have watched the Mosque grow under construction and now it is finished and we are here. A short drive from Salwa's house brings us to the parking lot, and we go directly to the visitor's changing room to put on traditional covering. I am given a blue garment with a hood, and Barbara is given a brown garment. Interestingly, in my heart I had wanted to wear blue.

The Mosque is all Light with shining marble inlay floors that appear to be a sea of white. Marble pillars with gold capitals flank the passageways.

There is a large open courtyard to receive the people. We make our way to large prayer rooms that have ornate chandeliers with amazing lights of color. Of special beauty is the marble niche with shimmering gold light.

Yes, the Mosque is exquisitely filled with Light. Its impact is so overwhelming that I hope to return again. I have no camera but I film the beauty with my eyes.

———————

When we return to Salwa's home, everyone is busy packing paintings to be transported to the Abu Dhabi Art Fair. I see beautiful paintings of landscapes with calligraphy featured as rainbows, clouds and light over cities.

In the afternoon, Salwa, her staff, and Maurice leave to set up the exhibit.

———————

November 6:

Salwa takes us to the Art Fair and it is still being assembled. It is exciting seeing the paintings. Some are so large, they can easily fill the large wall spaces of modern buildings.

In the evening, Maurice drives us to the airport for us begin the next part of our trip.

Barbara Wolf, Margaret Anderson

INDIA

We have been invited to attend the 18th International Conference of Chief Justices of the World held at the City Montessori School in Lucknow, India.

To reach India, on November 6 in the evening, we fly from Abu Dhabi to Mumbai, India, arriving 2:40 a.m. the next day. Now we must wait nine hours to fly to Lucknow, our destination.

I have been dreading this long layover until I see Mumbai Airport with its soaring architecture emphasizing the essence of Indian art and architecture – its vastness and intricacy.

I sit in the Gate 47 waiting room lounge looking at amazing light fixtures shaped in the form of tropical plants—closed to wide open. Lattice grillwork appears to be tropical and I can imagine fresh breezes blowing. Old Maharaja India style is here—spacious, opulent, and elegant.

We sit basking in this beauty and at the same time, we delight in seeing the women wearing saris—bright pinks and yellows and a whole range of colors and patterns. A delight to the eyes.

Just as we are basking in the beauty, Divino Roberto Verissimo of Brazil arrives. What a joy to see him!

Together, we take Jet Airways from Mumbai to Lucknow, a short flight. When we arrive, Shishir Srivastava's staff members are here to greet us and take us to the school guest house where we are given a fourth floor room overlooking a pool.

Then we have lunch, and then Shishir joins us and takes us to the auditorium where we meet Dr. Gandhi, founder and head of the school.

———————

76

November 8:

Because the conference has not yet begun, five of us are driving in a fancy van with purple curtains to a hospital because we want to understand the health services of the country. We will spend two days visiting city and country hospitals. The Chief Justices are sight-seeing where we have earlier visited, and so we do not want to revisit these places.

Now we take a long drive through Lucknow, crossing bridges and thruways and roads packed with motorcycles, tut tuts, trucks, cars driving on the left side of the road in British fashion. There are masses of motorists flowing, weaving, honking, passing, swerving on the road. It feels like a river or sea current is propelling the people along—workers going to work, children going to school—all crowding the roadways!!

Our first stop is at a government hospital with free medical service for the rural people. We are met and greeted by the staff and we walk up a long ramp to the next floor to go to the maternity ward of mothers resting with their just born babies. They are very quiet.

We approach with great smiles and greetings. Barbara and Roberto, who is with us, address each mother and newborn baby. The women respond with smiles to our greeting. Roberto praises the great care the mothers are receiving and the attending staff are pleased with our visit.

Our next stop is Saint Ann's Catholic Hospital but this hospital has only three patients and so we do not stay.

Next we go to the Gomti River to check on the condition of this river. For my conference talk, I will be speaking about the improvement of the condition of river by the government. When we stop at the river, I have miniature Vortexes in my hand. As the warmth of my hand touches the Symbols, these give out Love and Light to the river.

We three chant the OM's for the river.

I notice the river is barely moving. It seems to have lost its clarity and vitality. There are no birds, no animals near the river.

I hold tight to the Symbols as we stand by the river and chant the OM's for the water, for the trees, for the life forms. Praying nearby is a man wearing a prayer robe and turban.

Our driver now takes us to visit Sahara Hospital, a private hospital founded in 2009. We find it to be very modern. When we enter, we are greeted by the powerful statue of Bharatmata, Mother India. This Goddess rides a chariot pulled by four lions and she carries the flag of India. I feel her presence is a great protector of the people's heath and well-being.

Now we meet Administrator Aman Singh Chaudhary who takes us to the head of the hospital for an agreement that someone will show us the entire hospital. And yes, we are taken to all the departments from the entrance to where people check in to emergency, bone setting, rehabilitation, to the area of the MRI and CT scans, pharmacy, maternity. The rooms are often filled with daylight. Attentive staff warmly greet us.

I find the facilities to be impressive at this hospital. There is great space, accessibility, and order.

Humor and smiles are the best ways to exchange understanding and friendship. Later, Roberto invites Administrator Chaudhary to visit his homeland in Brazil.

It has been a fantastic morning filled with meeting exceptional staff. They opened their hearts to us and we responded.

November 9:

This morning we visit a government public hospital receiving 5,000 patients a day. If surgery is done, the patients can stay overnight or at another civic hospital with available beds.

The Director designates a staff member to take us on a tour of Admissions, Emergency, Cardiology, and the Women's Ward. We note the hospital staff are loving and compassionate even though there are hundreds of patients with family members.

We visit a very ill woman with her family and then we visit two men injured in motorcycle accidents. Their hands and arms are covered with bandages.

The number of patients needing help is overwhelming, and we admire the dedication and care of the staff members.

Later, when I write up my notes, I reflect on the loving concern and the kindness and care of those attending the great number of people needing help and medical attention.

On return to the City Montessori School, green parrots greet us by flying over our heads. We remember them from last year and maybe they are remembering us.

November 10:

Because of fog, the Chief Justices arrive late from the airport. They have been sightseeing in Delhi. We watch them walk slowly through a double line of welcoming students who are playing bagpipes and drums. Each student, wearing smiles, greets them by saying, "Good morning, ma'am", or "Good morning, sir".

All are gathered on the steps of the auditorium for a photo to be taken. 267 have come from 57 countries. The cameraman shouts, "One, two, three….Smile. A, B, C….Smile!"

Now, in the auditorium, the program opens with a United Nations type meeting of students debating climate change, one government, etc. It is an excellent presentation of the students.

In the late afternoon, outside on the school field, there is an elaborate cultural presentation of 7,000 students performing a vast variety of Indian dancing.

———————

November 11:

The morning session in the auditorium opens with prayers, singing, and speaking of students about problems facing the youth of the world. Then there are presentations by the Chief Justices and Heads of State.

In the afternoon, in adjoining conference rooms, Barbara and Roberto present their talks.

Afterward, our friend Shishir takes us in his car to the High Court of Lucknow, a vast judiciary complex. Here we are served elaborate high tea.

Then we go to dinner at the Lucknow residence of Yogi Adityanath, Chief Minister of the State of Uttar Pradesh. Before reaching his residence, there is a big traffic jam because Security is checking people entering the residence grounds.

As we are having our meal, the Chief Minister greets everyone and sits with Dr, Gandhi and his family. When we are eating, the FOWPAL (Federation of World Peace and Love) group from Taiwan dances the peacock dance and then they dance the happiness dance which is capped with a marshal arts performance.

All is upbeat. Dr. Gandhi's grandson joins the group and dances the horse and dragon dance. Roberto dances and Mrs. Gandhi embraces Barbara. Great joy is shared by all.

———————

November 12:

When we are attending the Chief Justice Conference sessions, we meet two young men from Germany, Erik and Tobias, who tell me how group singing in elementary schools increases brain development. I find this interesting. We also discuss differences in world music and how music systems in different parts of the world influence each other.

In the evening we are taken to a campus where the Taiwan people again show us their dancing. Also, Shishir's son plays Chopin music on the piano. Although he is young, only fifteen, he has great talent and we later learn he wants to study music in Germany.

————————

November 13:

Today I will be speaking on a panel whose topic is Creating a Culture of Unity & Peace. Chairman of the panel is H. E. Dr. Pakalitha B, Mosisili, Prime Minister of the Republic of Lesotho. Zhaklina Dimovska of Macedonia will also be on the panel.

To be settled for my talk, I arrive early.

When Prime Minister Mosisili speaks, I find him to be a kind moderator who addresses the students with respect and encouragement. In his country, his goal has been to have it mandatory that all children go to school from Primary to Grade Eight.

The custom was for young boys to attend the animals and not go to school. He saw to it that all children go to school so they would have a chance to be successful. They would not be held back and unable to cope with modern society. Usually, girls are kept at home, but in Lesotho it is the boys.

Dr. Mosisili honored the excellent world education found here at City Montessori School.

The other speaker, Zhaklina Dimovska of Macedonia, gives an excellent understanding of the nature of the human being. She says the body has four systems—physical, mental, emotional, spiritual. Cultures may be different but the key is for each person to have self-love. When there is Love of Self on the spiritual level, the individual cannot harm another because humans are all one. Her presentation is excellent and the students carefully listen to her.

———————

Here is my talk.

Cross-Cultural Understanding Helps Earth Healing

Specifically, I wish to speak about cross-cultural understanding that has come to different continents for the healing of Mother Earth. My talk begins with the Tibetan Buddhist monks now living in India who came to Rochester, New York State, July 1997, to present the teaching of the Kalachakra, The Cycle of Time.

In ancient times, this teaching was given to the public during intense times of great turmoil and chaos when peace was sorely needed. The teaching was aimed to bring unity, tranquility, and understanding to the people. This would transform the individual so as to bring peace within the self. Then, the individual would become a vehicle for transforming society as a whole.

During part of the teaching in Rochester, New York State, an elaborate sand mandala was constructed by the monks as they prayed and chanted. At the end of the teaching, the sand mandala was dismantled and carried to the Genesee River. Then it was poured into the water. This pouring would spread healing and blessings to the entire region.

I was present when the sand fell into the water, and it felt like a great burst of Light shot upwards. Powerful energy! This was amazing to behold. I felt the spreading of healing and blessings.

The next day, the Tibetan monks traveled to nearby Ganondagan, land considered sacred to the Native American Seneca Nation. Here, the monks gave blessings to the land as they continued the healing work of the Kalachakra teachings. I knew the monks also came to honor the kinship and friendship between Tibetans and Native Americans. The cross-cultural love and understanding was powerful.

Afterwards, I watched the healing energy and peace energy continue. A week later, as I was driving south through the mountains of New York State, I looked up to the sun. It was dancing, spinning, flashing yellow, red and white light. This was a holy sight! I felt the sun was reflecting the power of the sacred teachings brought by the Tibetan Buddhist monks.

For a moment, I felt the world had come together and I basked in the expansive energy of Peace and Unity.

A few years later, November 11, 2011, I attended a Native American conference called the Star Knowledge Conference. Here, Chief Golden Light Eagle of the Lakota Nation and Grandmother SilverStar of the Cherokee Nation gave to the people a sacred Vortex ring of twenty-two Universal and Spiritual Symbols. These are powerful healing symbols.

Barbara Wolf and I carried the Vortex Symbols to Lucknow when we participated in a four-day gathering called Confluence 2013. During this time period, we took the Vortex Symbols to the Gomti River which was polluted. Here, we listened to sacred music called Musical Rapture as I drew the Vortex Symbols on the riverbank.

Across the river we heard chanting by about thirty voices. How amazing that the chanters were doing the same work as we were doing! This was indeed a true cross-cultural healing for Mother Earth.

During our visit to Lucknow we gave the Vortex Symbols to a friend who placed them on his balcony overlooking the Gomti River. A year later, he told us that the government had begun working on cleaning the river. What a joy to receive this message!

I want to conclude my talk with you that members of the Nature Kingdom are aware of the healing energy of the Vortexes. One time while I was drawing the Vortexes on a beach in Hawaii, five whales breeched at the horizon.

Another time, I was drawing the Vortex Symbols at a large pond in Japan near a sacred Shinto shrine. With my mind, I spoke silently the symbols as I drew them. A small turtle began swimming toward me while I was speaking the symbols. When the last symbol was spoken, the turtle was at my feet.

And here is my final comment. One time I was in California to place Vortex Symbols at the Pacific Ocean. When I arrived at the beach, a Pacific seal was in the water waiting for me.

Look at the amazing energy of peace and unity and healing that can be spread around the world! Look at what you can do when your heart is in it!

With love,

Margaret Anderson

———————

After I give my talk I have an interesting discussion with students. The classroom is filled with over a hundred upper grade students—mostly boys. I enjoyed answering many questions because they were questions I already pondered.

One question was how do you do interfaith dialogue and I answered that I have experienced this at the Symphony of Peace Prayers at the World Peace Prayer Sanctuary at the foot of Mount Fuji in Japan. There, every May, religious leaders of the world's faiths come together to speak their prayers for peace. The audience, up to 10,000 people, hear these prayers and speak them. In doing so, each person realizes that all the prayers are the same no matter what religion. The basis is love.

———————

After my panel talk at the Chief Justices Conference in India, Shishir invites us to overlook Lucknow while sitting on an upper floor of the high Radisson Hotel Restaurant.

We have a wonderful meal with his family and the two Germans as we overlook Lucknow. I observe the city is heavily polluted and the view is dim. Yes, there is pollution in India.

We return to the school to rest for tomorrow's travel home.

————————

Later, I review today's events.

Zhaklina Dimovska says if you love yourself you will not go to war with another. All humans are the same on this planet. She also says, don't be a frog in a pond just sitting. Be an eagle and soar. See the world from above.

Chairman Dr. Mosisili tells about how a baby eagle was taken from its nest to a chicken farm and raised with the chickens. A man came and saw it was an eagle, not a chicken, and lifted the eagle up and told the eagle, "You are an eagle. Go fly." And the eagle did.

This morning while I am having breakfast at the pool, I see two butterflies dancing, spinning. One lands on the ground. A kind man picks it up and puts it on a wall so it will not to be stepped on. Kindness, everywhere.

————————

November 14:

As I am eating breakfast, nine green parrots are on an overhead line. They say, *Good morning world. Welcome to our world. Good Morning.* Later they comment, *when you are with Nature, Nature is with you.*

————————

When we begin our journey home, at the airport I meet a delightful woman, a psychologist, who works at the American Hospital in New Delhi. She has written the Book of Love. Her sister has written the Book of Joy. She is a good friend with Dr. Gandhi. As we are talking, local people are listening and they want to see the eBook (Memories 2017) I give her.

————————

When we return home, we write this letter:

Dear Dr. and Mrs. Gandhi and Shishir Srivastava,

Barbara Wolf and I have just returned to the United States after our participation in the 18th International Conference of Chief Justices of the World, November 8 – 14, 2017. The conference feeling tone was high, soaring—bringing the world chief justices, leaders, and guests together to address visionary ideals concerning the welfare and well-being of world children.

It felt as if we had reached the top of a high mountain where we all came to discuss, understand, share, and then put into action the vision of world peace and unity where all children could thrive and develop their highest potential.

Afterwards, on our long trip home to the United States, we talked about the conference. I am still euphoric about the joining together of people from all countries, races, religions focusing on the welfare of children. There was a great sense of brotherhood and sisterhood—a sharing of a common goal -- deeply held beliefs for passing the world to the next generations to make things better. All hearts shared the same focus. Different languages. different approaches. Same intent—the love of the children living in a peaceful harmonious world.

A gathering of dreams shared by all, thanks to you, Dr. and Mrs. Gandhi, Shishir, and all the dear staff at the City Montessori School.

With love and warmest greetings,

Margaret Anderson and Barbara Wolf

CHAPTER 10

New York City

From Barbara:

December 1 - 3 we will be in New York City to accomplish three goals.

1. To attend at Carnegie Hall a benefit concert performed by Tim Janis who is well known for his tireless efforts to help Mother Earth during this time of uncertainty.

2. To attend a program at the 9/11 Tribute Museum which will concentrate on patching religious differences so that another 9/11 will not happen.

3. Attending a Brooklyn Tabernacle gathering of 2,000 plus people singing with their hearts full of love.

But first we need to reach New York City. A taxi driver takes us to the train station which is newly opened. Fortunately, he knows how to reach the entry point where helpful train personnel are ready to escort us through the new boarding process.

First, we take an elevator down. Then we can either take an escalator up or another elevator up. When we use the elevator up, we reach the platform and soon the train arrives. Many of us are waiting to board and now we are told another new process.

Only pairs can board. This does not make sense until we are actually on the train and realizing that the seats are paired. Because the train will be so full, I realize that pairing can help the train staff to easily know when a car is loaded.

In any case, once everyone has boarded, the train moves slowly away from the station and our minds are on reaching the next stations, Syracuse, Rome, Utica, Amsterdam, Albany. When we cross the Hudson River after Albany, I examine the river from the window. Last winter there was so much ice, it seemed impossible for ships to be on the river. Well, there is no ice, but I see no ships.

I note that last year's evidence of algae is not here. Good! I know that authorities were using poison to kill it and I felt the sea creatures such as the sea gulls and ducks were also poisoned. Today I do not see any of them.

What continues to worry me today is the height of the river. The train tracks are so close to the river's edge and the river is so high, I feel that some day the train and water will meet. Goodbye using the train to reach New York City.

We arrive at our destination nearly on time, which I find amazing. When we reach the straight run from just after Albany to New York City, we travel along steadily without having to slow to a crawl when freight trains are near us.

I think the train tracks are the property of businesses carrying their products such as oil and gas. Passenger trains must allow them to pass. When we begin a slow crawl, our conductor tells us there is a freight train approaching.

The weather is beautiful today with bright sunshine and few clouds. It is December 1 and the snow has stayed away. This will make it easier for us to walk around New York City.

When we reach New York City, we stand in line with many other passengers waiting for an available taxi. The train had remained full throughout the journey and we realize now that the city is stuffed with people. Are so many here because they are shopping for Christmas?

A taxi comes for us and we begin crawling along the heavily crowded streets of traffic until we reach our destination, the Salisbury Hotel, which is practically across the street from Carnegie Hall.

Tonight at Carnegie Hall there will be a special benefit concert composed by Tim Janis, a friend of Mieko Sakai of Japan who is also our friend. A couple months ago he told Mieko that we should come to his concert because he knows we have great interest in helping Mother Earth. He also has that great interest.

Yes, tonight at 8 p.m. he will be performing a benefit concert called The Way of the Rain – Voices of Hope to help bring awareness of the need to protect Mother Earth. Tim Janis is well known for his tireless efforts to help where help is needed. For example, he worked with others to create Music of Hope, a way to raise funds for the American Cancer Society. Also, his music helped fund needed schools and he held concerts in China to help the Chinese people realize the beauty of America. The US State Department helped him give concerts in Eastern Europe to promote American goodwill. And he has worked with top musicians to promote Music With A Mission. His tireless work has led to one million music albums being sold.

Just before 8 p.m., our Japanese friend Mieko Sakai with her son meets us and we enter Carnegie Hall to watch Tim Janis' performance of The Way of the Rain concert. Many people are waiting to enter, and when the doors are open, we are directed to our seats close to the big stage. We know our view of the big stage will be perfect. As seats begin to fill quickly, I realize that all the 1,021 seats will be taken.

Musicians are filing onto the stage in front of me. They begin warming up by playing their instruments and I realize they are having a wonderful time doing this. Each plays his own music as people filling all of Carnegie Hall are talking and laughing and enjoying themselves.

When 8 p.m. arrives, I am wondering how this place with 1,000 plus people will become silent so that the performance can begin. No one is asking anyone to stop speaking. But, quite suddenly, about 5 minutes after 8 p.m., everyone stops talking. The musicians stop playing their instruments and Carnegie Hall is quiet.

Now I find it hard to explain what I am seeing—art and color combined with sophisticated music. I have never experienced what I am looking at.

It is an example of Tim Janis, whose sophisticated brain has put sight and sound together to show us his concept of the formation of Mother Earth and all on her.

First, the art and music combine as chaos. This is to indicate the lack of order during very, very ancient times.

Then there is a BIG BANG—the birth of the Universe. Then the Milky Way is formed and the Earth appears. We see water, air and the moon. Even the fairies are evident. And the trees. This leads to what is happening just now, a great forest being cut down. Then a great fire. Yes, Tim Janis is showing us what we are experiencing now.

At the end, we see rain, and this indicates hope.

Now comes dialogue between N. Scott Momaday and Robert Redford, important devotees of The Way of the Rain. They meet on stage and the two sit in dialogue for several minutes to show the audience that talk among individuals helps normalize the problem of misuse that Mother Earth is undergoing just now. As they talk, we listen.

And now it is time for former Vice President Al Gore to speak to us. He is author of bestseller Earth in the Balance, and he explains the need to tell the world about the danger of climate change.

December 2:

Tim Janis has invited us for breakfast at 9 a.m. at Le Pain Quotidien. We New York City foreigners do not have a clue where this place is but our hotel manager tells us to walk out the hotel door, turn right, and then right again, and then do this and do that. Well, with hope in our hearts, we begin walking and asking. Fortunately, this place is well known, and within less than ten minutes we are there.

Mieko, our friend from Japan, soon arrives, and shortly after 9 a.m. Tim Janis arrives. The place is crowded but a narrow table is furnished for us. I sit exactly across from Tim Janis. On either side of him are a husband and wife from Iceland. How interesting. A few years ago, the quickest and least expensive way to reach Europe was to fly from New York City to Iceland, stay overnight, and the next day fly to Europe. When my husband and I had an art gallery in America, we flew once or twice a year using this method to buy European art for sale in our gallery.

Well, in Iceland, I only had a chance to speak briefly with Icelanders, and now two of them are sitting on either side of Tim Janis. What fun to talk with them!

As for breakfast, I am looking at the menu and not knowing what to order, but Tim Janis makes a suggestion. He says he will order a bread basket. Would Margaret and I like to share this with him? Yes, even though we have no idea what is in the basket. Well, the order was fine and the breakfast was fine.

Tim Janis cannot stay long because he has artistic appointments in Connecticut and then Massachusetts, etc. Yes, that man is a busy man.

————————

Mieko Sakai has told me that she and her son will be attending a holiday program at the 9/11 Tribute Museum today at 1 p.m. She wants Margaret and me to come. Well, yes, of course. We know nothing about this 9/11 Tribute Museum but we know about 9/11, the moment in 2001 when a terrorist attack by Muslims brought down the World Trade Center in New York City. My investigation of the Internet told me that 2,996 were killed and 6,000 injured.

I went there soon after the attack to send out Peace, Love and Light, and I saw firemen still fighting a fire there. People visiting the site were giving the firemen paper prayers to put on a large wooden cross.

For the 2001 disaster, I did not know there are numerous memorials. One of them is the 9/11 Tribute Museum in New York City. This would be the location of today's program. In charge will be Buddhist Reverend Dr. T. Kenjitsu Nakagaki who for many years has focused on bringing peace. At today's meeting there will be Buddhist, Christian, Jewish, Hindu, Muslim and other religions.

About an hour before the program begins, we take a taxi to the 9/11 Tribute Museum. Arriving here is a surprise. This is a normal looking city building squashed in with other normal looking business buildings. I had never expected this.

When we enter the building, we realize we are in the visitor's reception area and we are told to take the elevator to the second floor, etc., etc. After leaving the elevator, we become a bit lost, but then we come to a room where teenagers are sitting at a table concentrating on making paper peace lanterns. We have arrived!

Shall we make lanterns? Yes. And so we sit down to make them. When mine is finished, I am shown how to make it into a shape of a lantern, a peace lantern. A bead of light is put in it and then my candle is placed with about twenty other finished lanterns.

The museum has put a beautiful photograph on the Internet showing a lighted candle beside big water. I remember one year when I helped make lanterns in Hiroshima that were floated down a river. Is the museum intending to do something similar with the candles we are making?

Representatives of various religions are coming into the room and standing near the lantern table. They are Buddhist, Christian, Jewish, Muslim, Hindu, etc. Mieko introduces me to Reverend Dr. T. Kenjitsu

Nakagaki who has obviously invited the other religious leaders. They begin speaking with each other in a quiet, friendly manner. Some speak a few words to us about the need for peace.

I am happy to visit this small tribute to 9/11. I never expected to attend this meeting that stemmed from intense negativity. It is so different from yesterday's Carnegie Hall concert and yet both are important for all living on Mother Earth.

————————

December 3:

Yesterday, we check out of our hotel near Carnegie Hall to go to Brooklyn to stay at the Sheraton Hotel which is less than a five-minute walk to the Brooklyn Tabernacle where we will listen to hundreds singing with their hearts wide open at a Sunday 9 a.m. service. Two times earlier we have been caught being late for the service, and so we have learned that we must pay attention to weekend work on the metro. I think that fewer people take the metro on weekends and so, on weekends metro repair work is done. Without warning, metro lines are closed. This weekend we will stay at a hotel close to the Tabernacle!

And yes, Sunday, December 3, we arrive early at the Tabernacle, and we file in with great numbers who have also arrived early. They know that seats can be filled and what is left will be in the rear. Margaret and I find four seats with a good view of the Tabernacle stage, the location for the choir. Two seats are for Mieko and her son, and we hope they will not be late.

As we are sitting and watching the Tabernacle fill up, we have our hands ready to shake those who are coming to greet us with their hands out and smiles on their faces. It is so wonderful to be with such warm, giving people. Peace, Love and Light. Peace, Love and Light. If everyone in the world could be friendly like the ones in the Tabernacle, that would end negativity.

Now it is close to 9 a.m. and Mieko and her son arrive. This is the first time they have visited the Brooklyn Tabernacle and they are wonderfully surprised to feel the joyfulness of the place.

At 9 a.m., the choir takes the stage to sing. There are about 270 voices. Promptly, the audience is asked to sing with them and we all burst into song. Mieko, who is beside me, is laughing and laughing as she sings. I do not think she has participated in such a joyful manner of singing.

When the first song is finished, we immediately begin singing another. Some in the audience have their arms high above their heads, swaying with the music. Mieko puts her camera to her face to take a photograph and a smiling tabernacle attendant tells her no. I have forgotten to tell Mieko that photographs cannot be taken.

When we finish singing, the pastor begins talking with us. He has a strong positive way of talking and it is like he is speaking to each of us individually. We listen and listen and listen and he talks a long time. Then we are asked to sing again and we do.

Yes, being at the Brooklyn Tabernacle this morning is exactly where I needed to be to send Peace, Love and Light out to the world, and I do.

Again, here is what I wrote at the beginning of this chapter:

(1). The Carnegie Hall concert emphasizes the need for rain to bring our planet into balance.

(2). The 9/11 Tribute Museum program brings religious faith into harmony with each other.

(3). The voices at the Brooklyn Tabernacle sing in harmony with each other for the planet.

CHAPTER 11

New York City

From Margaret:

December 1:

The train ride to New York City is enjoyable because so many happy people are riding it. We meet a brother and sister originally from Malaysia and we learn they have not seen each other for forty years. They are sharing their joy with everyone.

In New York City, our taxi driver from Penn Station to our hotel is from Ghana who is discouraged about the American dream. He wants to go home. He tells us Americans used to be nice but now they are tense and selfish. They are not the kind, generous people he knew when he first came to America.

The Salisbury Hotel where we are staying is comfortable and there is great advantage to staying here. It is a two-minute walk to Carnegie Hall where we will be tonight watching a remarkable art, film and music concert—The Way of the Rain—Voices of Hope.* This event was created by environmental artist Sibylle Szaggars Redford and composer Tim Janis.

*See Glossary: The Way of the Rain – Voices of Hope.

We have a mutual friend, Mieko Sakai of Japan, who is also a good friend of Tim Janis. When Tim Janis learned that we are devoted to working for the benefit of Mother Earth, he said we should come to Carnegie Hall to see tonight's performance.

When the tickets went on sale, I phoned the box office and asked the ticket seller what would be her favorite seats in Carnegie Hall. She said Parquet J113 and J114, and so we booked these tickets immediately. They are just the right distance from the stage and on the same level as the stage. We will have comfortable seats.

Mieko Sakai and her son Daisuke have come to New York City to attend the concert. They meet us at our hotel at 7:30 p.m. and we go together to Carnegie Hall. Concert time is 8:00 p.m. and we see many waiting for the doors to open. When this happens, we are nearly the first to enter and we go to our seats to wait for the performance to begin.

I am very exited to see this performance. On the stage will be the Chesapeake Youth Symphony Orchestra and youth choirs from Mount Olive High School, High Point Regional High School, and Howell High School. Also on stage will be musician composer Tim Janis as well as Native Americans, African Americans, and Celtic performers.

The concert starts with a great explosion of a combination music and art to represent the creation of the Universe. Then we go from Darkness to Light. The Sun is created and we discover Earth approaching with one moon.

The art and music become a tribute to Mother Earth. We are bathed in the TOTAL BEAUTY of the trees, the waterfalls, the oceans, the rainbows, the grasses, the prairies, the mountains. All are bathed in Love. Everything grows and evolves in Love—integrated into the perfection of the whole of the Universe.

My eyes start crying when I see Earth appearing on the great wall behind the orchestra and choir. Carnegie Hall has become a film screen. Delicate architectural details highlight the natural structure of Nature. Shimmering gold leaf wall decorations harmonize with details of Nature on the screen. Then the film sadly turns to the issues of deforestation, wild fires, hurricanes, volcanoes, droughts, etc. Often they are manmade. A great feeling of hopelessness enters.

Now Al Gore comes on stage speaking about HOPE. He is followed by actor and environmentalist Robert Redford and Native American poet N. Scott Momaday. They share deep respect for each other's culture as well as honoring and supporting vibrant Nature on Mother Earth.

Native American flute player and singer Robert Mirabal has brought his three daughters with him and an Eagle Dancer to present the Native American honoring of Nature.

Robert Mirabal lives attuned to the streams of water currents in the air that affect the weather conditions. He says these currents have to be addressed and honored in prayer.

In my opinion, The Way of the Rain – Voices of Hope is indeed a SPECTACULAR art, film, and music concert. I leave full of hope.

————————

December 2:

I am up early, still ecstatic about the grand performance, and I begin reading last night's program from cover to cover. I read the biography of each soloist, each artist, each filmmaker. Also, I read about Tim Janis, the Redfords, Al Gore, etc.

Later, I scour the Internet for information on this performance, as well as all the artists and performers in order to circulate among my friends and family the wonder of this musical event.

————————

We are told that Tim Janis will meet everyone at breakfast at a restaurant called Le Pain Quotidien. Here, we find Tim to be completely delightful and he is pleased about our excitement over last evening's performance. We give him our book, Memories 2017, and we tell him that his concert will be noted in our next book. He orders breakfast for us and we enjoy eating with him before he has to leave to go to Connecticut for a next performance.

_____

After breakfast, we return to the hotel to pack our bags and leave them at the front desk for a late pickup. At noon Mieko and her son go with us to the 9/11 Tribute Museum that commemorates the event of September 11, 2001.

Here, we join a group from different faiths making peace lanterns to be put later in a pool or river near the museum. Today's museum event has been organized by Reverend Dr. T. Kenjitsu Nakagaki, Japanese Buddhist priest who is a good friend of Mieko. Many families are here to participate in today's museum event.

Barbara and I sit at a large table with children making paper peace lanterns, using bright colored pencils. I love being with the little girls drawing decorations of Peace and Love on their lanterns. I draw May Peace Prevail On Earth on four sides of a lantern and surround the words with flowers and bright suns. When each lantern is finished, it is placed on a decorative cloth with symbols of different religions.

Our host, Reverend Dr. Nakagaki, leads the group in prayer. He is a gentle soul. Other religious leaders of different faiths are here to give prayers for world peace, love and healing. I feel peace rising up from this event and spreading across the city and the world. Even though everyone comes from different parts of the world, at this moment all hearts become united as one.

When we leave the 9/11 Museum, we take a taxi uptown to pick up our bags, and then we cross the East River to Brooklyn to stay at the Sheraton Hotel which is near the Brooklyn Tabernacle where we will be tomorrow.

_____

December 3, Sunday:

We have an early breakfast at the hotel and then we go to the Brooklyn Tabernacle,* arriving early, and finding seats in the second row of the middle section. This has a good view of the stage which the choir uses. Soon Mieko and her son arrive and sit with us.

*See Glossary: The Brooklyn Tabernacle.

When the chorus of nearly three hundred begin singing, the music is very powerful and the congregation joins in with their hands stretched up to Heaven. All hearts are open. Everyone is caring and compassionate. Love abounds.

When the pastor begins his sermon, he tells us about the helpful volunteer caretakers of the church and the mission of the church. He also tells us about a new Bible arranged in chronological order to tell the Christ story.

After the service is over, we say goodbye to our dear friends Mieko and her son and we walk back to the Sheraton. Here we pick up our bags and go to Penn Station to take an early afternoon train home.

On the train back, as we are traveling up the Hudson River, the scenery of the train ride is filled with GOLDEN LIGHT. I think of the Hudson River School paintings of earlier times that captured the same Light. I watch the mirror reflections of the trees in the water. It feels like filming the Spirit of the River. When the sunset begins, the sun appears with golden clouds surrounding it. This caps off an amazing weekend.

GLOSSARY

CHAPTER 1: MOUNT SHASTA

The Lemurian community of Telos beneath Mount Shasta.
Mount Shasta: http://www.mslpublishing.com/pages/Mt-Shasta.html
Telos, Volume 1, 2, 3. http://www.mslpublishing.com/categories/Books/

Blessings Chimes, gift of David J. Adams of Australia.

David J. Adams: http://www.dolphinempowerment.com/MarineMeditation.htm
https://soundcloud.com/david-j-adams

Star Knowledge Vortexes and Universal Symbols:
SilverStar, THE SYMBOLS, THE VORTEXES, http://starelders.net
http://www.starelders.net/store.htm

Chief Golden Light Eagle, THE SYMBOLS: http://www.
starknowledgeenterprises.com/the-symbols/

CHAPTER 2: SOLAR ECLIPSE

Songlines: Australian Aborigines - Indigenous Australians ~ History,
http://www.crystalinks.com/aboriginals.htm

Relaxing Music, Relaxing Meditation Music "Flower Canyon"

by Tim Janis. https://www.youtube.com/watch?v=1GHryf7WctU

Horse Sculpture, Sundown Hill, Australia,
The Broken Hill Sculpture Symposium, Yegor Korzh.
https://www.yktravelphoto.com/places/the-broken-hill-sculpture-symposium/391

CHAPTER 3: SACRED FIRE ~ SACRED LAKE

Emma Kunz, https://www.emma-kunz.com/en/emma-kunz/

CHAPTER 4: HEALERS AND SPIRITUAL BEINGS

AIONA A, Swiss Healing Rock Powder,
https://www.emma-kunz.com/en/aion-a/

CHAPTER 5: YELLOWSTONE

James Tyberonn, Earth-Keeper Chronicles,
http://www.earth-keeper.com/ek-chronicles-channel-information/

CHAPTER 7: KOREA

JAMES TWYMAN: TWO MAJOR UPCOMING SYNCHRONIZED
MEDITATIONS:
http://toc-now.com/james-twyman-major-upcoming-synchronized-
meditations/

Beethoven, Ode to Joy:

Beethoven - Symphony No.9 (10000 Japanese) - Freude schooner
Götterfunken (Video)
https://www.youtube.com/watch?v=X6s6YKlTpfw

Pat and Frank Hunt's work with the Korean Refugees.
http://peaceworks.afsc.org/patricia-hunt/story/326
http://peaceworks.afsc.org/frank-hunt/story/327

CHAPTER 8: UNITED ARAB EMIRATES AND INDIA (Barbara)

Sheikh Zayed Grand Mosque Abu Dhabi, http://www.idesignarch.com/sheikh-zayed-grand-mosque-abu-dhabi/

CHAPTER 11: NEW YORK CITY (Margaret)

The Way of the Rain Voices of Hope Carnegie Hall, December 1st, 2017 World Premiere (Video).
https://www.youtube.com/watch?v=k2YQAt8mm1Y

Visionaries:
Tim Janis, Producer Composer, Artists, Poets, Orchestra and Chorus, Robert Redford, Sibyville Szaggars Redford, Robert Mirabal and Family.
https://www.facebook.com/thewayoftherain/photos/a.1413009675635716.1073741825.1413008155635868/1982722305331114/?type=1&theater

View of Stage:
https://www.facebook.com/thewayoftherain/photos/a.14130121123022139.1073741827.1413008155635868/1989590234644321/?type=1&theater

Children's Choir: https://www.youtube.com/watch v=GPZ76WAhP1o

The Brooklyn Tabernacle: http://www.brooklyntabernacle.org

VORTEX SYMBOLS

Chief Golden Light Eagle and Grandmother SilverStar have given us valuable information on how to use powerful energy fields to help Mother Earth and all that live on her. This information has come from sacred ceremony and the information is available through:

1. THE SYMBOLS. The Universal Symbols and Laws of Creation: *A Divine Plan by Which One Can Live.*

Original title: MAKA WICAHPI WICOHAN, Universal & Spiritual Laws of Creator. [The 11:11 Symbols Book] By Standing Elk © 1996]

2. THE EARTHSTAR WAY 13-Moon Calendar, The Universal Symbols and Laws of Creation in Day by Day Living.

3. THE VORTEXES. The Universal Symbols and Laws of Creation.

http://www.starelders.net
http://www.starknowledgeenterprises.com/the-symbols/

Here is more explanation on the Vortexes and Symbols:

Two Star Law Symbols combined make one Vortex.

The **Vortex of Light, Sound and Vibration** is formed by joining the

Symbol of the *Universal Law of Light, Sound and Vibration* with the Symbol of *Spiritual Law of Intuition.*

The **Vortex of Integrity** is formed by the *Universal Law of Free Will* combining with the *Spiritual Freedom of Man*. This is a free will planet and can only operate fully when there is complete spiritual freedom of man. There should be freedom with truth and honesty.

The **Vortex of Symmetry** is formed by combining the *Universal Law of Symmetry* with the *Spiritual Law of Equality*. Symmetry means balance between all things, both spiritual and material. As above, so below. Also, equality between male/female, left/right brain, etc.

The **Vortex of Strength, Health and Happiness** is formed with the combining of the *Universal Law of Movement and Balance* with the *Spiritual Strength, Health and Happiness*. In life one has to be balanced to move forward and also one has to move forward to be balanced. Balance is symmetry in motion. With movement and balance come strength and health and happiness.

The **Vortex of Right Relationship** is produced by combining the *Universal Law of Innocence, Truth and Family* with *Spiritual Protection of Family*. This is also a powerful Vortex of social relationship (based on truth) when the concept has moved from the individual to the group.

The **Vortex of Growth** is formed when the *Universal Law of Change* is combined with the *Spiritual Growth of Man*. Change is a basic tenant of life. With spiritual growth, all things thrive. All things change. Nothing is static. Therefore, both the individual and society need the spiritual growth of man. When humanity grows spiritually, then the Vortex of Growth flourishes. In the natural state, all things grow unhindered. With spiritual growth all things thrive.

The **Vortex of True Judgment** is formed by combining the *Universal Law of Judgment* with the *Spiritual Law of Karma*. All actions should be looked at through the eyes of the *Universal Law of Judgment* so that no harm is done and there is no karma. The latter, the consequences of action, can be turned into dharma, teaching. This law applies socially as well as environmentally.

The **Vortex of Perception** is formed by the combining of the *Universal Law of Perception* combined with the *Spiritual Law of Future Sight*. It is important to perceive the impact of one's actions and to use the gift of future sight. Needed now are planetary actions that affect in a good way the lives of the people in relationship to the air, the water, the land, the life on this planet.

The **Vortex of Connection to Life** is formed with the combining of the *Universal Law of Life* with the *Spiritual Law of Choice*. Life is enhanced by correct choices. It is diminished by poor choices. Therefore, choose wisely. Choice and Life are integrally connected.

The **Vortex of True Nature** is formed by the combining of the *Universal Law of Nature* with the *Spiritual Law of Protection*. Nature exists and thrives. It is up to mankind to protect Nature so that all life thrives on this planet.

The **Vortex of Love** is formed by combining the *Universal Law of Love* with the *Spiritual Law of Healing*. One has to have Love to give healing and to receive healing. Love is the greatest healer. People, Nature, all creatures, plants, cells, molecules, atoms, adamantine particles respond to Love. All have a consciousness. Love creates. Love heals. Love is the highest power of all.

A Vortex is formed at the center of a circle of all Vortexes displayed together. This Vortex is called **Universal Unity and Spiritual Integrity**. All Vortexes bring unity. All Vortexes thrive with integrity. Integrity is the foundation of the Vortexes.

Printed in the United States
By Bookmasters